THE GOD-ORDAINED LIFE:

EMPOWERING YOU TO MAXIMIZE YOUR GOD-GIVEN ABILITY TO OVERCOME ANY CHALLENGE

BISHOP JAMES C. AUSTIN, SR.

LIFE TO LEGACY, LLC

DEDICATIONS

I want to dedicate this book first of all to the Almighty God who planted the seed of faith in my heart many years ago and made me tire of meetings that talked only about how bad things are. I resolved in my heart that I did not want to sit in another committee meeting that was not about solving problems.

After all, you know the definition of a committee, don't you? A committee is a group of people who get together to discuss problems and decide that NOTHING CAN BE DONE!

Lord, please, deliver me from such committees! The only committee I want to be a part of is one that ends its meetings with an ACTION PLAN. For crying out loud, at least plan a prayer meeting if you can't think of anything else. DO SOMETHING! There has to be something we can do! THANK YOU, LORD! You are the greatest!

Second to God is my wife, Vernesta—the love of my life! It was she who showed complete confidence in my ability to write a book and who, when she saw me working so hard to make several network marketing projects succeed for the people I serve, would say to me, "Honey, the time you are spending on these projects is time you could be spending writing your book!" She was a constant voice and a consistent encourager for me to complete this book.

Thank you, Darling! I appreciate you so much for giving me the time and space to do this. Also, HAPPY MOTHER'S DAY! I cannot wait until May of each year to say that. Because you are such a good mother every day of the year, you deserve to hear "happy mother's day" often. You have mothered for me four adorable children. Though grown, they have developed talents and professions that are a tremendous credit to you.

Thanks also to my children, James Jr., Dorcas, Prisca, and Marcus, for making Mom a joyful mother and me a proud father! I pray that God will continue his work of perfecting you, stablishing you, strengthening you, and settling you in His perfect will (1Peter 5:10).

ACKNOWLEDGMENTS

Thank you, Corey Young, for helping me with the pictures for this book! Thank you, Letricia Dixon and Dr. Carol Collum, for your diligent review and editing of my rough drafts!

Thank you, Bishop Carlis L. Moody and Mother Mary Moody for your unfaltering friendship, counsel, and guidance for more than 40 years! Bishop, you married Vernesta and me 40 years ago, and we are still keeping our vows, loving God, and loving each other. Thanks again!

Finally, thank you members and friends of the St. Luke Church of God in Christ, who, each week, attend the Sunday and Midweek Bible studies on the Northside of Chicago to hear me preach and teach the principles and plans of God! Your constant prayers and expressions of love have been an ever-flowing fountain of support to me. I pray God's favor over your lives.

FOREWORD

There are many books written on HEALING and RECOVERY, most of which focus on how to make you feel better after having a traumatic experience. I don't want the readers of this book to walk away simply feeling better, because this is not meant to be a pacifier. But rather, I want you to BE BETTER. Lord, deliver me from the doctor who focuses more on my symptoms than on my underlying problem.

I was visiting a patient in the hospital, and the doctor said to the patient in my presence, "Push the button if you experience pain or discomfort because I can do something about your pain. However, I cannot do anything about the real problem that will eventually take you out. This is a PAIN CENTER! Thus, I can keep you reasonably comfortable. There is no need for you to suffer—or at least no need for you to be aware of your suffering. I can do something about that!"

Is that what you want? Is that the news you look for from your primary doctor? Is FEEL BETTER all you want, or do you want to BE BETTER?

This book is designed to give you REAL ANSWERS for REAL PROBLEMS, and the ability to bounce back from the most horrific, traumatic experiences. It is not filled with meaningless theories and human imaginations, nor suggestions to change Personality Traits, but rather, it is filled with wisdom from above—God-given wisdom taken from His Holy Word and from life experiences. It clearly establishes that it is possible to change your direction and bounce back. There is no wisdom anywhere superior to that which is recorded in the Holy Scriptures.

My wife, Vernesta, and I visited Philadelphia, Pennsylvania, several years ago and stopped by the historic Holy Temple Church of God in Christ, which was presided over by the world-famous preacher and bishop, the late Bishop O. T. Jones, Jr. Since I had not made an appointment to see him, I expected at most to be able to say, "Hello, we are visiting from Chicago and we simply want to see this historic church."

What a surprise! He stopped what he was doing, walked us into the sanctuary, and said to me, "Brother Austin, there is a story in the Bible for every experience you have ever had, are having now, or will ever have! Learn the stories of the Bible!" He further said, "If you preach to hurting people, you will always have people to preach to."

After thirty years, these words continue to resonate in my spirit and have helped me get through some very difficult times. They have also helped me help others get through difficult times. You are about to be blessed because you will find your experience somewhere in this book, as well as a biblical process for turning trial into triumph through your God-ordained life.

–Bishop James C. Austin, Sr.

TABLE OF CONTENTS

CHAPTER 1
LESSONS FROM THE HAWAIIAN TREE

THE STORY

While visiting the Big Island of Hawaii, I took a long walk by the Pacific Ocean and passed many trees on my left and on my right. Of all the trees, one tree caught my attention more than others.

I saw a tree growing up out of the ground for only a few inches, then it took a downward turn toward the ground. Most trees grow straight up for several feet before they turn or branch out, but something happened to this tree in its early development that caused it to turn prematurely towards the ground and to grow parallel to the ground.

It appeared that this tree was meant to be deformed, impaired, disabled, and subordinate to all trees for the rest of its life. For from its inception out of the ground, it could not keep its head up and grow up like other trees.

But I noticed that after a good distance of parallel growth, there was a bend in the branch. It was as if the tree reasoned within itself to say, "I was not meant to grow like this. I am better than this. God ordained me to lift my branch toward the sky, and that is exactly what I am going to do."

At the point where the bend was, I saw the branch curve upward toward the sky, never again to bow itself to the ground. Once there was a change in its direction, it remained lifted up to the sky, bearing beautiful flowers and leaves.

But I also noticed that this tree had some help in its quest to reach up to the sky. I saw several places where someone had chopped branches away from the tree. These were branches that possibly would have weighted the tree down to a low position and prevented it from reaching its maximum potential. The tree received help!

APPLICATION

We cannot change our date of birth, our place of birth, our birth parents, our siblings, our residency at birth, or the dysfunction of our families. We can do nothing about who reared us, who had a strong influence on our lives, who controlled our actions, or who protected us and kept us out of harm's way.

Moreover, we cannot change the abuse we experienced as children. We had nothing to do with giving ourselves a name. For years, we were at the mercy of others. But at some point in our maturity, we made a decision that would correct the direction of our lives permanently. We experienced a bend toward God and His righteousness, and we will never revert to the old person we were before.

SCRIPTURES

> Therefore if any man be in Christ, he is a new creature: old things are passed away; behold, all things are become new.
>
> 2 Corinthians 5:17

> [1] I am the true vine, and my Father is the husbandman. [2] Every branch in me that beareth not fruit he taketh away: and every branch that beareth fruit, he purgeth it, that it may bring forth more fruit. [3] Now ye are clean through the word which I have spoken unto you. [4] Abide in me, and I in you. As the branch cannot bear fruit of itself, except it abide in the vine; no more can ye, except ye abide in me. [5] I am the vine, ye are the branches: He that abideth in me, and I in him, the same bringeth forth much fruit: for without me, ye can do nothing.
>
> John 15:1–5

In order to increase the growth and quality of the fruit the branch bears, the husbandman purges (cleanses or cuts away) those twigs or branches that will prevent that tree from growing to its full potential. In like manner, there are some family members and friends whom God has assigned to our lives for a season, but He does not intend for us to take them into our future. So at some point, He cuts them away from us.

As you embrace wholeheartedly the word of God, some family and friends will fall away from you. Do not grieve too much over this, for God is preparing you for your future, and these persons are not meant to be a part of that future.

I have also observed the removal of family and friends for a season, and then a return of some of them at a later season in life. So leave all things in God's hands; He knows and sees the future clearly.

CHAPTER 2
THE LIFE-CHANGING "BEND"

We oftentimes become frustrated and upset when we are in an uncomfortable place too long. Especially when we cannot see an end to this troubling experience, we tend to lose hope that anything will change for the better. It is at this juncture that we must pull out the book of faith and call for some testimonies, for "the testimony of the Lord is sure, making wise the simple" (Psalm 19:7).

JOB was sick so long until the flesh fell from his bones. He lost all his cattle and children. In the end, everything that he had was gone. Yet, in the midst of all of his despair, Job fell down on the ground and worshipped God, saying, "Naked came I out of my mother's womb, and naked shall I return thither: the Lord gave, and the Lord hath taken away; blessed be the name of the Lord" (Job 1:21). The Bible goes on to commend Job for the outlook he had during his trial. It says that "in all this Job sinned not, nor charged God foolishly" (Job 1:22).

Job was so very sick that he thought of dying. In the 14th chapter of his book, he raised the question, "If a man die, shall he live again?" Then he responds to what appears to be an irreversible dying process with these words: "all the days of my appointed time will I wait, till my change come" (Job 14:14).

In the 19th chapter, Job expresses his faith in God, proclaiming,

> 25 For I know that my redeemer liveth, and that he shall stand at the latter day upon the earth: 26 And though after my skin worms destroy this body, yet in my flesh shall I see God: 27 Whom I shall see for myself, and mine eyes shall behold, and not another; though my reins be consumed within me.
>
> Job 19:25–27

Job maintained a steadfast faith in God, while waiting for his change to come. And although many years passed before he heard from God, Job waited!

APPLICATION

Isaiah 40 expands upon the benefit of waiting on the Lord, "They that wait upon the Lord shall renew their strength; they shall mount up with wings as eagles; they shall run, and not be weary; and they shall walk, and not faint" (Isaiah 40:31). Strength comes through waiting on the Lord. The ability to soar to new heights comes through waiting on the Lord. Wait, I say, on the Lord! Your change is coming!

From birth, I grew up in a Pentecostal church. Our church is highly charged emotionally. In other words, we have good church.

It is exciting because the members are demonstrative praisers. When Dr. John MacArthur of California visited Chicago for a book signing, he said to me, "We Evangelicals need more of what you have. Your church has spontaneity!"

He is right! When you come to my church, you don't know from one minute to the next what is going to break out. We believe in letting the Holy Spirit have His way and encouraging the Spirit to move us however He wants to. In fact, I grew up hearing the statement, "I wouldn't have a religion that I could not feel."

While that statement sounds good to us Pentecostals, there is a downside to it. For, if we walk by feeling, we will be gravely disappointed. We must walk by faith and not by sight or feeling. We must be able to trust the Lord when we cannot feel his presence.

That is the problem I have with the song, "Every time I feel the Spirit moving in my heart, I will pray!" My friend, we must pray when we do not feel the Spirit moving in our hearts. Jesus spake a parable on this wise, "that men ought always to pray and not to faint" (Luke 18:1).

Paul told the Thessalonian church to "pray without ceasing" (1 Thessalonians 5:17). You must live in a state of prayer at all times. Pray when you rise, and pray when you retire. Pray as you go, and pray as you return. In all seasons of your life, PRAY! For "the effectual fervent prayer of a righteous man availeth much" (James 5:16). It may be a long time coming, but change is going to come.

Habakkuk 2:3, 4b reads:

> [3] For the vision is yet for an appointed time, but at the
> end it shall speak, and not lie: though it tarry, wait for it;
> because it will surely come, it will not tarry … [4] the just
> shall live by his faith.

Go to the end of the book of Habakkuk and look at the faith
and confidence that this prophet had in God in the face of an
economic collapse:

> [17] Although the fig tree shall not blossom, neither shall
> fruit be in the vines; the labour of the olive shall fail,
> and the fields shall yield no meat; the flock shall be cut
> off from the fold, and there shall be no herd in the
> stalls: [18] Yet I will rejoice in the Lord, I will joy in the
> God of my salvation. [19] The Lord God is my strength,
> and he will make my feet like hinds' feet, and he will
> make me to walk upon mine high places.
>
> Habakkuk 3:17–19

Habakkuk was in touch with his God-ordained self and
found safety and a strong sense of security in the Almighty God.
Situations which should have unnerved him and caused him to fall
to pieces could not affect him to the same negative degree that
they affected others. For God was his hope. He had no one else to
look to for survival and victory over this deplorable circumstance.
God was his only resource.

Please note that Habakkuk began praising God in the midst of his grim economic forecast.

> [18] I will rejoice in the Lord, I will joy in the GOD of my salvation. [19] The Lord God is my strength …"
>
> Habakkuk 3:18–19

Through the prophet's actions and attitude, I hear him declaring, "God holds the promise of my future. My destiny is in his hand. I will come out of this a victor because The Lord will turn my captivity around." Habakkuk did not sound pitiful and depressed when thinking of the Lord God as the only answer to his dilemma.

So do not lose your grip on who you are and whose you are during seasons of distraction and poor prognosis. The God-ordained life is God-conscious and can always be found dwelling "in the secret place of the most High and [abiding] under the shadow of the Almighty" (Psalm 91:1).

Did Job's change come?

> [10] And the Lord turned the captivity of Job, when he prayed for his friends: also the Lord gave Job twice as much as he had before. [12] So the Lord blessed the latter end of Job more than his beginning: for he had fourteen thousand sheep, and six thousand camels, and a thousand yoke of oxen, and a thousand she asses. [15] And in all the land were no women found so fair

as the daughters of Job: and their father gave them inheritance among their brethren. [16] After this lived Job an hundred and forty years, and saw his sons, and his sons' sons, even four generations. [17] So Job died, being old and full of days.

Job 42:10, 12, 15–17

Thank God, Job's change came! And I write unto you to tell you that your change is coming!

NEXT WITNESS

JABEZ was a lonely, rejected person who was labeled at birth to be a lifetime failure. There is no record of his father. Chances are that he grew up without paternal support.

Thank God for mothers because they are natural nurturers! But poor Jabez was not blessed with this. Jabez did have a mother, but she was never able to release the memory of the extreme pain he caused her in childbearing. She most likely suffered from what we call today postpartum depression syndrome. As a result, she named her son Jabez, which means pain.

Throughout his developing years, his mother, his family, his neighbors, his schoolmates, and his teachers called him pain because his Mom called him that both publicly and privately. When he came out of his mother's womb and experienced her rejection and disapproval, his spirit had to be as flat to the ground as the

Hawaiian tree. He was destined to be a gang leader, a drug addict, a jailbird, or a very bitter and angry terror to humanity.

He was daily confronted with extreme rejection on every hand. People seemingly did not want to be bothered with him. They excluded him from events and activities in which his peers readily participated. He could not find acceptance anywhere except in the synagogue.

I am sure that Jabez could identify with Rudolph, the red-nosed reindeer, who was ignored and scorned. If you've ever been in a state of rejection, you understand how Jabez longed for acceptance.

Boys and girls, men and women do extremely foolish things to gain acceptance from their peers. Oftentimes girls become promiscuous in hopes of finding acceptance and affirmation, but instead find themselves dealing with an unwanted pregnancy and low self-esteem. Guys seeking approval will do wild and crazy things at the demand of their peers.

Imagine Jabez as a child growing up and watching children his age being picked up by Dad and hugged by Mom. Jabez wanted so much for his mother to show some affection, but it wasn't happening. Out of desperation, he probably thought, "Well now, if Mom cannot hug me, will somebody show me some love?"

It would have been easy for Jabez to say, "You just wait until

God blesses me. I am not giving you guys anything." Instead, he prayed to the God of Israel:

> Oh that thou wouldest bless me indeed, and enlarge my coast, and that thine hand might be with me, and that thou wouldest keep me from evil, that it may not grieve me! And God granted him that which he requested.
>
> 1 Chronicles 4:10

I am inclined to believe that a Rabbi or a teacher in the synagogue took time with Jabez to teach him the word of the Lord. There he learned the stories of Jacob and the testimonies of God. While he had no spiritual or emotional support at home, he found spiritual and emotional nourishment in the synagogue. The word of God resonated in his spirit, and there he saw his way out of his dilemma.

So Jabez called upon the name of the God of Israel. Why the God of Israel? Maybe Jabez identified with Jacob (later called "Israel"), who was despised, rejected, and hated by his twin brother, Esau, so greatly that Esau devised in his heart to kill Jacob. Jacob ran away to save his life.

Jabez, I am sure, felt like running away but did not know where in the world to run. At least Jacob had some relatives to whom he could run. Jabez had none. Yet, with all the support of his uncle, Jacob still felt alone, mistreated, cheated, and totally disadvantaged, destined to not become the God-ordained person he was meant to be. Under his uncle's wings, Jacob was cramped and unable to fully express himself. He needed to return home, and he needed God's favor to do so, for his brother, Esau, was waiting on him there.

One day, Jacob decided that enough was enough. It was time for a "bend" in his life. So, he gathered his wives, Leah and Rachel, his children, his servants, his cattle, and took off from his Uncle Laban's farm. When he was getting close to his destination, he stopped to spend some time alone with God. It was then that he encountered an angel.

Jacob grabbed the angel and would not let him go. Jacob so desperately needed God that when the angel said, "Let me go for the day is breaking," Jacob replied, "I will not let thee go, except thou bless me." The angel then asked him his name, and Jacob said, "Jacob." The angel told him that he would no longer be called Jacob, but that his name would be "Israel: for as a prince hast thou power with God and with men, and hast prevailed."

Even after the angel disabled Jacob by disjointing his thighbone, Jacob held onto the angel and would not let him go. Jacob desperately needed God's presence and favor if he were to continue his God-ordained path. Because of his unshakable faith in God, his request was granted. Jacob was able to meet his brother, Esau, in peace and live in the same land with him in harmony. What a blessing!

Jabez picked up that faith and called upon the name of the

God of Israel, saying, "Oh that thou wouldest bless me indeed, and enlarge my coast, and that thine hand might be with me, and that thou wouldest keep me from evil, that it may not grieve me!"

In other words, Jabez was saying, "I've got some relationships I need you to fix. So the same way that you blessed Jacob, bless me, Lord. Do to me what you did to Jacob. My name is pain. Please change my name. But if you never change my name, change my circumstance. Make me honorable among my brothers. Let them see your hand upon me. Make ways for me to enlarge and increase, despite the disfavor I have been shown by mother, family, neighbors, and peers. Lord, You make something beautiful of my life.

"God, I so desperately need You. I envision a God-ordained me that is very different from the perception others have of me right now. If I continue on the path Mom has set for me, I will be the low, lonely product of her imagination. People do not have high expectations of me. They have already written me off and classified me as unfit and unprofitable for life.

"But I see a different me. I see myself expanding, growing, and blessing others, governing and supervising thousands of people. I see myself owning many cattle and employing many servants. I see myself in charge of many things, which my Mom and my teachers could not see in me. They have written me off, but You, Lord, can write me in. I, being in touch with my God-ordained me, am praying to You, God, for favor, and for Your hand of mercy and grace to be upon me.

"Now in order for me to stay on the God-ordained track, I must not let evil trip me up or cast me into a snare. So, Lord, keep me from evil. Keep me from a bitter spirit that can lead to hurting somebody, for hurt people hurt people! Lord, keep me! Please, Lord, I feel like hurting those who have said some cruel things to me and about me behind my back. Please, Lord, keep me!"

APPLICATION

Just as Jabez found answers to his dilemma in the synagogue, youth are coming to the church today from very troubled homes, looking for a way out of their dilemma. The God-ordained members of the church must be ready at all times to address their deepest concerns.

Romans 10:13–15, 17 teaches the process of effective faith and the importance of faithful teachers:

> [13] For whosoever shall call upon the name of the Lord shall be saved. [14] How then shall they call on him in whom they have not believed? And how shall they believe in him of whom they have not heard? And how shall they hear without a preacher? [15] And how shall they preach, except they be sent? As it is written, How beautiful are the feet of them that preach the gospel

of peace, and bring glad tidings of good things! [17] So then faith cometh by hearing, and hearing by the word of God.

God is looking for the people He has ordained to be the teachers and preachers who will engender faith in the hearts of those in despair, hope in the hearts of the hopeless, strength in the minds of the weak, love to the unloved, and relief to the thousands of people all around us who are plagued with grief. Those who are God-ordained and Christ-centered have the answers to the world's ills. So give it away!

"Righteousness exalteth a nation, but sin is a reproach to any people" (Proverbs 14:34). Keep me, Lord! Hold me! Do not let me sin as a result of my bitter experiences. Hold me, Lord, and keep me from sinning against you and sinning against my fellow man. Keep me, Lord!

Oftentimes rejection causes people to seek acceptance and love in the wrong places. The results can be devastating. Lord, keep me from evil. Keep me from going in the wrong direction, mixing with the wrong folk, for evil company corrupts good manners. Keep me, Lord, that it may not grieve me or cause me to become bitter toward people whom I deem myself justified to hate. Lord, keep me!

"And God granted him that which he requested." GOD created a "bend in the road" for Jabez. He was never the same again. The scripture 1 Chronicles 4:9 declares that Jabez was more honorable than his brothers.

I can only imagine that the God-ordained life of Jabez included a beautiful wife and lovely children. He who was once undesirable became most desirable. He who was once unattractive became very attractive. He who had very little now had very much. God turned things around for this little unsung hero because he believed on the God of Israel. Jabez called on the name of the God of Israel, and God granted him that which he requested.

What a mighty God we serve! I see a bend coming in your life as you do what Job did. He humbled himself before God and prayed for his friends before he ever realized his own deliverance. He held on to his integrity even when he could not sense God's presence.

You must cleave to the Lord as Jacob did and not let Him go until He fulfills His promises to you. That is called holding on by faith! God "is able to do exceeding abundantly above all that we ask or think, according to the power that worketh in us" (Ephesians 3:20).

Finally, sidestep negative energy and ugly things that people say to you or about you. Stay focused on the development of your God-ordained life. God is moving you along a path that will astound those who know you now. He is bringing you into a wealthy place, a large place. Can you believe that?

Several years ago, I was in Dallas, Texas, to preach for a National Evangelist Department breakfast when I heard a children's choir sing. This was an evangelistic service being held at the Honorable Bishop J. N. Haynes' church. Everything was geared toward evangelism.

The founder and coordinator of this choir introduced the children as ones that the school system had written off as incapable of learning or ever becoming productive to society. This dear lady developed a school with these special children in mind. The children were very disciplined and orderly in their presentation. One child eloquently rendered excerpts from a Dr. Martin Luther King, Jr. speech and was received with adoring applause from the congregation. Then one of the children announced that the choir was going to sing one selection. "The title of this song is 'Cheerios'."

I thought to myself, "This is an evangelistic service. Evidently, someone failed to let the dear lady know this before she brought these precious children here." Since I had directed children's and teen's choirs since I was twelve years old, and at one time had one of the best children's choirs in Chicago, I expected to hear them break out into three-part harmony with a contemporary gospel song or at least "Jesus loves the little children—all the children of the world." But, no, the song these children would sing was "Cheerios".

I watched them go into their gospel choir rock, swaying side to side. And then came the sound of their voices in unison. "Cheerios, Cheerios, you may push me to the bottom of the bowl, but I'll rise to the top." They repeated these same words about eight times and went to their seats. There was no verse to the song, just this simple chorus.

I looked around the audience. No one was dancing in the aisles. No one was shouting from the pews. But I saw Kleenex and handkerchiefs being used to wipe tears from many eyes. Reluctantly, I pulled my handkerchief out to act as if I needed to wipe sweat from my face. (After all, men don't cry!)

The truth was that I understood for the first time the true meaning of evangelism: to meet needs and heal hurts. I also realized that those children had stolen the show with their "Cheerios" song.

Honestly, I cannot remember any other participant that night, and there were several. The only memory of that night is that of those dear and precious children who had been redeemed by someone with vision. Someone had instilled Philippians 4:13 in them, "I can do all things through Christ which strengtheneth me."

So, push me to the bottom of the bowl, if you will. I'll rise to the top, because I am a "Cheerio"—a God-ordained being!

CHAPTER 3

YOU ARE APPROACHING A "BEND" IN YOUR LIFE!

While working as a manager for the Social Security Administration (SSA) several years ago, I was sent to a seminar for managers on the topic "You Are What You Were When." It was a course designed to help us understand the people with whom we work and to enable us to help employees cope with their personal concerns so that their personal issues would not adversely affect their work performance.

I remember a film we were shown. It was a brief lecture on the same topic by Dr. Morris Massey from the University of Colorado-Boulder. Basically he said that we are products of our environment. The community of people surrounding us during our developmental years directs and greatly determines the course of our lives. If something does not come along and shake us or move us to do something different from what Mama did or what Grandpa did, we will fall into the same traps and ruts that most of our family members and close friends from the same community fell into.

Dr. Massey said that oftentimes we need a Significant Emotional Experience (SEE) to take place in our lives in order to influence a major change. He said that everyone needs a compelling reason to change, and a SEE will do it.

My mother experienced a SEE in the spring of 1978. My mother watched several of her peers move into senior residences, and she was so glad that she and my father had purchased a conveniently located house on the south side of Chicago in 1954. While she was not lifted up with pride, she was proud to have a place she could call her own. Never in her most distant dreams would she have considered moving out of her most comfortable home, in which she had invested so much money, time, and energy. Mom was set for life!

In 1978, Dad, who had been pastoring the St. Luke Church of God in Christ ever since he founded it in 1942, was enjoying being able to observe the growth and development of his four grandsons, Joe, Lydell, and Samuel (by my brother, Luke, and his wife, Tina), and James Jr. (my firstborn with Vernesta). But for years, my mom longed for a daughter. Well, on March 25th, a daughter finally came in the form of a granddaughter when my wife gave birth to Dorcas.

My wife's first day back to church after the birth of our daughter was on Sunday, May 7th. My father, after officiating over Communion, added to the order of service the blessing of our daughter. He held her in his arms and prayed for her, not knowing that two days later he would go to sleep and not wake up. Around midnight on Tuesday, the 9th, Mother called me and said, "Get over here as soon as you can. Something is wrong with Dad. He is not responding to me." Well, that's all she had to say. I lived less than a mile from them. My wife and I quickly got ourselves together, jumped in the car, and drove speedily to their house.

Trying to be the cool, calm thinker, I called Dr. Parson, a physician who lived just two doors north of Mom. I thought he could make it over to the house quicker than emergency personnel summoned through a 911 call. In a few minutes, he was at her door. He did the two or three tests that doctors do to determine if there is still life, then he looked at me and said, "Dad is gone. You can call the mortician to come and remove him."

I heard what the doctor said but still asked in disbelief, "Shouldn't I call 911 so that he can be taken to the hospital for emergency care?" Dr. Parson calmly said, "No, Dad does not need to go to the hospital. I am a board-certified physician. You can call the mortician now." After a few seconds of silence, I accepted the reality of the moment and called Brother Ernest Edwards of Golden Gate Funeral Home.

Dad, who had preached and blessed my daughter on Sunday, the 7th, who was at the prayer meeting and talked with me in the vestibule of the church for several minutes while the saints gathered on Monday, the 8th, who as far as any of us knew had no particular physical challenges on Tuesday, the 9th, was pronounced dead a little after midnight! This was totally like a dream to me and difficult to accept.

Vernesta and I made two or three calls to the nearest relatives and leaders of the church. After that, the sad news was relayed to others through chain calling. Several relatives and members of the church came to the house in the middle of the night to comfort us and to see what they could do to help. I was amazed at how quickly they formulated the program, the obituary, and the order of service, making everything flow within the next three days.

Do you realize how many months we spend planning a major event? But here in three days, a team of leaders planned a funeral attended by more than a thousand people and made all things come together in an orderly manner. I simply marvel at this effective synergy.

Dad was laid to rest on Saturday, the 13th. The late Bishop F. G. Green came to St. Luke on the following day, which was Mothers' Day, to officiate that first service after Dad's death and to get a feel for the wishes of the St. Luke family.

When he announced to the church that he was contemplating placing the young son of the founder as pastor of St. Luke, without hesitation an overwhelming majority of the church stood up, clapped their hands, and praised God. Bishop Green then said, "Based on your immediate response, I think I will put him in position right now. Come up here, my Son."

I was standing off to the side of the church by the piano. After all, I was the minister of music, happily serving wherever I could.

I, at thirty-two years old, did not have a clue that this new weighty assignment was coming so soon. I approached the podium where Bishop Green was standing, and he laid hands on me, prayed for me, and presented me to the St. Luke Church family as the pastor. Talk about a SEE! This was certainly a SEE for me.

I knew that I could not work full time at the SSA and simultaneously be effective as a pastor of this well-established church. So, I went to work the next day and announced that I would be resigning in two weeks. Those two weeks went by so fast, because I spent very little time at work. I used some of my saved personal time to deal with transitional tasks related to the church and bringing closure to some tasks at SSA. My SEE changed my occupation.

I oftentimes say that I went to the University of Illinois-Chicago (UIC), majored in biology, minored in chemistry, and ended up in ministry. I do not regret the time I spent in those science courses, for they gave me an intellectual base to understand information given by medical practitioners: I have been better able to help families sort out their options and make critical decisions, oftentimes, knowing the questions to ask that family members so burdened with life and death issues cannot think to ask. My academic training has helped me walk families through critical moments in their lives. So, nothing has been wasted.

So Dad was gone. However, I was not alone because I had a wife and two children at the time. But what about Mom? Dad's sudden death was a major adjustment for her. Learning to live alone after almost fifty years of marriage was no small task for her. She now had concerns about safety, travel, management of her property, payment of bills, and all the responsibilities that Dad once took care of.

For me, it meant that I had to be at her house almost daily, making sure that she was okay. It meant checking in with her more often to see that she made it home safely from church.

Thank God for her spiritual daughter, Sister Earlean, who often picked her up, took her to church, and drove her back home! Sister Earlean would not simply drop Mom off, but she would get out of the car and assist Mom into the house. She made sure that Mom was in the door and secure in the house before pulling off.

On one occasion a couple of years later when Sister Earlean approached the front door as she accompanied Mom home from Sunday night service, she noticed that it was partially open. She quickly guided my mother back to the car and called the police because it appeared that someone had broken in while they were at church.

The police came. Sure enough, someone had broken into our family home and turned furniture upside down. You can imagine that Mom's secure world was shattered. Her heart was broken. She could only weep and weep and weep, for she felt so violated. How could someone prey on a senior citizen and destroy everything for which she and her husband had worked so long? How could any sane person do a thing like this? If Dad's death was not a big enough SEE to get her moving from her secure, comfortable home, this was. She was ready to downsize and do whatever was necessary to get into a more secure environment. It took less than two weeks to get her moved.

Do you know anything about moving? Have you ever had the experience of having to downsize after accumulating stuff over a lengthy number of years? Were you amazed at how much stuff you had to deal with in the move? Well, it's a blessing when you are moving from a small place to a much larger place, but moving from a large place to a much smaller place is a trip. You have to decide what to leave or give away, for you cannot take everything with you. But it is so hard to say goodbye to yesterday!

Mom had to make the decision of what to carry and what to leave. Oh my God, how difficult that was! I had to tell her, "No, Mom, that furniture will not fit in your new apartment; only this will." Has anyone been through this decision-making process?

Well, we finally got her moved. Amazingly, she showed no remorse for the old address. That SEE was so traumatizing that she seemed happy to put that bad memory behind her. One of our members was the manager of a new senior building that was in walking distance from the church. He was able to get her in at the beginning of June. She lived there until Bishop E. Lenox, Prelate of the Southern Illinois Jurisdiction, swept her off of her feet and took her to be his bride for the last few years of his life—another major SEE in her life. At seventy-five years old, my mother was married again.

Am I talking to a widow or widower who has said, "Praise the Lord, I do not see another marriage in my future. I am satisfied as I am"? Am I talking to someone who has said, "I am too old now to think about stuff like that"? Why do I feel like I'm prophesying to someone? I see a "bend" in the road for you.

STORY

Abraham, can you help me? I am stuck! Would you tell me what happened to you concerning this "too old" business? Are we ever too old to experience the powerful energy of GOD? I need some help because I'm communicating to thousands of people who feel like their time of blessings has passed and that there is no need to hope any longer. A spirit of discouragement has swept over the church community, and we have an unprecedented percentage of members in deep depression and in need of medical attention. They are stressed out over what appears to be a dismal future.

Some of these persons are not super old. One brother just told me that life is so difficult for him right now that he sometimes does not want to live. He wishes that he could go to sleep and not wake up, for everyday is a new challenge for him.

My father taught me a long time ago that the darkest hour is just before the dawn! He taught me to believe God in the dark!

The Lord awakened me one Sunday morning and said to me, "Jimmy, if you can hold to me in the tensest moment, I will bring you out of any situation victoriously." I said to God, "Lord, would you repeat that?" And he said to me again, "Jimmy, if you can hold to me in the tensest moment, I will bring you out of any situation victoriously."

Needless to say, I got up that Sunday morning ready to have church. I felt empowered to get the victory on the left hand and on the right. This was like a "bend" in the road for me.

All right Abraham, I know I have kept you waiting to give your testimony while I rambled on, but your story is so much more fascinating than mine. I hear that you were good at eighty-five years old. Do you know what I mean Abraham?

"Yes, Brother Austin, I have had at least several of those SEEs of which you are speaking. I didn't know back then what I was having, but you are teaching me something. What do you call it? A Significant Emotional Experience? The SEE that I'm speaking of started with something that came out of my wife's mouth one regular, routine day when she said, "Honey we need to talk."

I replied, "OK, when?" She said, "Now!" I said, "OK, let's do it." (The mindset of the man is let us do it now, whatever this is, and let us get it over with quickly. Better now than later!)

So, I sat down at the kitchen table and said, "OK, what's on your mind?" Then came the shocker. "Honey, I know you want a son, and I want what you want. But you are eighty-five years old and I am seventy-five years old. I have never heard of a woman having a baby at this age. I am not sure that I am even strong enough to have a baby now, but I know how much you want a son."

I tried to interrupt her conversation by saying, "Oh, Baby, don't worry about that. I'm happy with you. We can simply grow old together and enjoy each other. Whatever God has promised, He is more than capable of performing. Let's leave the baby to GOD!"

But my wife said to me, "I know we should trust God for His promises, but maybe He wants us to use what we have to make this happen. Instead of sleeping with me tonight, I want you to lay with Hagar, our handmaid and Egyptian slave, and whatever happens, well, let it happen!"

"Sarah, Sarah. Baby, you must be out of your mind. Did you make a mistake and drink something you should not have? Do you know what you have just proposed to me? Take Hagar and do what?"

My wife repeated herself and made it crystal clear that she was sane and in her right mind. Again, she said, "I want you to take Hagar. I have already briefed her, and she very shyly and reluctantly agreed to do this, because she knows that this is a very awkward setup in that she has respected you as the dad of the house for so long."

I said to her, "Are you sure you trust me to do this? Are you sure she even wants to do this? Are you sure that I am able to do this?" She emphatically replied, "Yes!"

I sighed and then reasoned within myself that if I had approached Hagar without my wife's permission, I would have been greatly rebuked, but this proposal is coming directly from my wife. Wow! I did not believe it.

How does an eighty-five-year-old man get ready at a moment's notice to intimately connect with a woman fifty years younger? Brother Austin, I'm not familiar with the new language you are giving me, but I think this was both a "BEND" and a SEE. Man, I never thought it could be until it happened to me.

Let me hasten to say that evidently I was younger than I thought I was, because something happened to me that night, and less than a year later, I was the father of my firstborn, Ishmael.

Maybe, I am talking to a man who fathered a child after he was sixty-five years old. You would understand the attachment that an old man has to the child of his old age. Oh my God, as far as I was concerned, Ishmael could do no wrong.

So when Sarah would complain to me about Ishmael, I would

take up for him. Actually, Hagar, a strong African mother, did an excellent job of caring for and supervising our son. I did not have to chastise him much because his mother was on top of everything, making sure that he did what he was supposed to do.

Now, Brother Austin, I thought I had had all the "BEND" and SEE I could stand, but at ninety-nine years old, I was visited by three angels who announced that Ishmael was not the son that God promised.

The angels asked me, "Where is Sarah, your wife?" I said, "In the tent." And the angel said to me, "I will certainly return unto you according to the time of life; and, lo, Sarah thy wife shall have a son." And Sarah heard it in the tent door behind him.

Now, Sarah and I were old and well stricken in age; and it ceased to be with Sarah, after the manner of women. Therefore, Sarah laughed within herself, saying, "After I am waxed old, shall I have pleasure, my Lord being old also?" She probably that, "At eighty-five, he was good. But between then and now, he has been stricken with old age. Things he used to do, he can do no more!"

And the Lord asked me, 'Why did Sarah laugh, saying, Shall I of a surety bear a child, which am old? Is anything too hard for the Lord? At the time appointed, I will return unto you, according to the time of life, and Sarah shall have a son.' Sarah was ashamed and tried to deny that she laughed, but the angel rebuked her.

What can I say, Brother Austin? It came upon a midnight clear, bright shining as the stars, that something happened and now I know he touched me and made me whole. One year later, Sarah was holding her own biological baby son. She was ninety years old, and I was a hundred years old. Do not tell me what God cannot do! I have experienced Him and know that He can do anything!

Brother Austin, how many of these SEEs can a man take? Because One day when I went into the house to enjoy the son of my strickened old age, my wife says again those words that most men dread to hear, "Honey, we need to talk." I reluctantly said, "All right, Darling, what is it now?"

"That fourteen-year-old son of yours must go. I caught him laughing at my baby, and I will not tolerate that in this house. Either he has to go, or I have to go. Which one, Abraham? Which one?"

"Has your wife ever pulled you aside and said, "We need to talk"? Oh my God, when she says those words, you know what goes through a husband's mind: "Lord, have mercy! What now?"

Usually wives do not warm us husbands up for what the conversation will be about. We are often hit by surprise. If there are any wives hearing my testimony, you might want to prepare your husband for what is on your mind. Some of this stuff can make a man go into a cardiac arrest."

Imagine Jacob married to this *Ebony Magazine*-front-cover-pretty girl named Rachel. One day she pulled him aside and said, "Give me a baby, or I die!" Jacob said, "What? Give you a baby or you what? I'm doing everything I can do. I don't make babies; God does, and I am not God. What in the world do you expect me to do?"

Are there any husbands out there who can identify with this? After you do all that you know to do to satisfy her, it's still not enough and you come short of resolving the issues of her heart. Then you can relate to the dilemma Elkanah found himself in when his wife sat over in the corner of the house weeping.

Men do not like being around weeping women! It pulls too much on their uncontrollable emotions. Have you heard the saying men don't cry? We are tough! We go into battle believing we can conquer anything. But then when we come home and find that we cannot master a simple matter at home, we are unraveled and made to feel less than competent. It goes against the grain of our masculinity. We feel as though our wives ought to be able to tell us what they need or are missing, and we ought to be able to do it or produce it. When they expect us to do what we cannot do, that makes us feel horrible.

Let us eavesdrop in on Elkanah's emotionally-charged conversation with his wife Hannah in the first chapter of 1 Samuel. "Ah, Hannah, Baby, what's the matter with you? Why are you here in the Shiloh Motel in the corner weeping so? Why are you so depressed? I noticed that you are not eating. This is not normal behavior. Why is your heart so heavy? Why are you so grieved? Am not I better to you than ten sons?"

Hannah, realizing that she should not make her good husband feel like he should take full responsibility for her misfortune, said little in reply. She got up, wiped her face, and ate. The grief, however, was still with her. So she went to the house of the Lord, where she could pour out her heart to God.

It was there that her strict, sanctified pastor, Eli, mistook her to be drunk. He said to her, "Woman, how long will thou be drunken? Put away thy wine from thee!"

Hannah immediately responded, "No, my lord, I am not drunk; I have not had any intoxicating wine to drink. I am a woman of a sorrowful spirit, and I am here pouring out my soul before the Lord. I know that he understands me when no one else does. I know that he will redeem me when no one else will. So, I am here pouring out my soul to him who is able to give me relief. Please count not thine handmaid for a daughter of Belial. Don't look at me as a wicked woman; for out of the abundance of my complaint and grief have I spoken hitherto."

Pastor Eli then said to Hannah, "Go in peace, and the God of Israel grant thee thy petition that thou hast asked of him." Hannah arose, and went her way. Her countenance was no longer sad. She encountered a "bend" in the road! She still did not have the baby, but she had a promise from the Lord, and that was enough to put a smile on her face. The fulfillment of that promise did come a year later, and her reproach was removed.

God answered Jacob's prayer. Rachel did eventually have a son named Joseph, and later gave birth to another son, Benjamin. God answered Hannah's prayer and gave her Samuel. God showed that he does answer the effectual, fervent prayers of the righteous.

All women are not the same; they do not all react to reality the same way. In the heart of a woman, there are unfulfilled desires, and they are communicated in different ways.

Abraham continues by saying, What does a man say when his wife forces him to choose between her and his child? Well, I tried to reject my wife's request by declaring, "Ishmael is my son, and he will stay with us until he is grown."

I am a meek and mild-mannered man who hardly ever acted tough with my wife, but this time I felt like I needed to put my foot down. Even mild-mannered men sometimes feel like they need to play hardball with their wives, especially when what the wife is bringing to the table is in serious conflict with the husband's desires.

As it turned out, I tried putting my foot down, but the Lord had me to pick it back up. I was tormented over the choice I had to make, but the Lord said unto me,

> [12] Let it not be grievous in thy sight because of the lad,

and because of thy bondwoman; in all that Sarah hath said unto thee, hearken unto her voice; for in Isaac shall thy seed be called. [13] And also of the son of the bondwoman will I make a nation, because he is thy seed

.

Genesis 21:12–13

Hearken unto her voice? Do what she demands me to do? This is a huge pill for a man to swallow, but not impossible, especially if the Lord has made a promise that all will be well!

So the next day, I did as the Lord commanded and brought peace to my house. Dealing with this SEE in my life was difficult, but it was good for me and for both sons. It all worked out.

All right, Brother Austin, let me finish my story because I do not know how many more of these SEEs I can stand. My wife lived thirty-seven years after giving birth to Isaac. She had a chance to see her child grow up and become a fully responsible grown man. She was so proud of him and glad to have the other boy gone so that her son could inherit everything.

But she died at 127 years old, and I had to bury her [out of my sight]. I was 137 years old when I had to say goodbye to my lifelong partner. Even though there were times when we disagreed on issues, somehow we were able to remain committed to each other until the end.

Sarah was the love of my life. This SEE left me alone with my son. Even though he was grown, I still felt somewhat responsible for him, for he had not married yet. I noticed that after his mother's death, he was not as cheerful as he had been. He seemed to be falling into a state of depression. I needed to find a wife for him.

I know you say, "Why doesn't he find his own wife?" But I just told you that I felt responsible for him. So I sent my servant to find him a wife, and he did. What a beauty he brought to my son! Rebekah was the very person he needed. He immediately perked up and was comforted by her arrival. Isaac was forty years old when Rebekah came to us. And it took them twenty years to have their first sons, Esau and Jacob.

Shortly after my son was married to Rebekah, I had another SEE! Brother Austin, I know this is hard to believe, but, at 140 years old, I felt new energy surging through my body. I thought I was stricken with old age at a hundred years old, but oh my God, a pretty country girl set me on fire again. I knew that I had to do the right thing with that fire. So I asked her to marry me. Would you believe she agreed to marry a man who was 140 years old?

I know you are saying that either she was stone crazy or she must have needed a father in her life. You may even be saying that it was her joy just to care for an old man like me until he died. Well, whatever you have to say about her, she became my wife, and I was able to amaze her with my fire.

Not only did I marry her, but we were blessed to start a whole new family. Keturah and I became the proud parents of six boys.

I lived thirty-five years with Keturah, enjoying the growth and development of our six sons.

Before my time to depart this life, I was able to give each of the sons of my super-old age something to get them started on their own. Then I sent them all away to the East Country, away from Isaac, my son of promise.

APPLICATION

When there is conflict in relationships, we need to maintain a proper attitude until we can get to a "Bend" in our interactions. When it appears that we are getting nowhere in our conversations with someone we love dearly, we must never lose hope and abruptly walk away. We will approach a positive "Bend" in our understanding if we lean heavily on God's wisdom.

Women are gifted with emotional sensitivity. They may not be able to always make sense of what they feel because sometimes all they know is that they feel uncomfortable. The more a man learns to listen to and interpret those feelings, the more complete he will be in his personal life and in the decisions he must make as the head of the household.

There is a dysfunction which takes place when the woman uses her feelings to dominate the relationship, making the man a puppet on a string who dances when he's not happy, laughs when he's not tickled. She must find a way to communicate effectively with her husband, allowing him to maintain his lordship over the household. Never should either spouse put the other down in front of other family members. Notice that each time Abraham had a conversation with his wife, Sarah, Hagar never interfered because she was not a part of it.

Not all problems can be solved the same day. It can take days, weeks, and even months before solutions can be found for some problems.

A brother called me late one night and said, "Pastor Jimmy, my wife and I are having an argument, and we cannot come to an agreement. What should we do?" I turned over and looked at my watch, then told him that it was about two a.m. and they both needed to shut down their mental computers, get some rest, and call me later. I trusted that they would be able to come to a decision after they had rested awhile.

How foolish it is to make a vow to argue it out no matter how long it takes and to not go to bed until an agreement is reached. I would suggest arguing until you finally agree that you are tired and need to take a break. Do not put yourselves through unnecessary pressure and stress. You will most likely live to see another day and be afforded the opportunity to complete what you could not complete the day before.

Your life is about to go through a major transformation. Do not worry. It is going to be good for you. For every good and perfect gift comes from above. God has commanded a blessing on your life, and what God has blessed, no man can curse.

God, speaking through the prophet Jeremiah said, "For I know the thoughts that I think toward you, saith the Lord, thoughts of peace, and not of evil, to give you an expected end" (Jeremiah 29:11).

No matter what you have been through, you have something good for which to hope. What is to come is better than what has been. God speaking to his servant Moses said, "Behold, I send an Angel before thee, to keep thee in the way, and to bring thee into the place which I have prepared" (Exodus 23:20).

CHAPTER 4
THE GOD-ORDAINED LIFE

When Adam was created, he was placed in the Garden of Eden for a specific, God-ordained purpose. Adam never had a day in which he pondered why he was here. From the very beginning, he knew his God-ordained purpose.

Adam's God-ordained life consisted of a man bearing the image of God and walking in His likeness. Just as God was the governor of the earth, Adam would govern the earth. Just as God had dominion over the fish of the sea, the fowl of the air, the beasts and cattle of the field, and all the earth and everything that creeps upon the earth, Adam was to have that same dominance. God even left the naming of all the animals to Adam. Thus, as God, Adam was a thinking, creative being.

God made Adam out of the dust of the ground and breathed into his nostrils the breath of life, and Adam became a living soul, according to Genesis 2:7. That living soul possessed the image and likeness of God.

The psalmist declares in Psalm 100:3 that "It is he that hath made us, and not we ourselves; we are his people, and the sheep of his pasture." We are forever subordinate to the Almighty God and can never take His place. No matter how much we are like Him, we can never BE HIM.

I am told that there was a famous scientist who told his students that they no longer needed to use God as a crutch. According to Him, man was capable of doing anything that God can do, including making man.

One day he announced to his class to spread the word that he was going to prove his point. "Tell everybody to meet me in the main auditorium on campus two weeks from today. I will have one pile of the finest black dirt delivered to that hall for God and one for me. If God can make man, I can too."

Well, that day finally came, and the auditorium was filled to capacity with students and faculty alike. As promised, there was a huge pile of dirt on the left side of the stage for the scientist and a huge pile on the right for God.

When the courageous scientist stepped out on stage, the audience raised a loud shout of praise for him. He had been so convincing in his written and verbal communication that people thought maybe he had an edge on other scientists and medical professionals. The people waited with great anticipation.

He said to the audience, "This pile is my dirt, and that pile is God's dirt," then once again boasted that he was capable of doing anything God does. Picking up a handful of dirt and slowly letting it fall down to the floor to prove that it was real dirt, he said, "Let us begin."

The scientist then picked up another handful of dirt, but before he had the opportunity to add water to it to make clay, God, placed His hand on the scientist's hand and said, "That's my dirt! I made this dirt! Get your own dirt!"

The scientist was paralyzed, unable to function. He had encountered divine interference. The crushed scientist dropped the handful of dirt on the floor and announced that he could not continue the planned exhibition.

But before the audience could leave, God interrogated the scientist. "Mr. Scientist, why did you give me a pile of dirt in the first place? Obviously, you do not understand the power of Genesis 2:7, which says that I "formed man out of the dust of the ground." There is a big difference, Mr. Scientist, between dirt and dust.

"You build houses and skyscrapers on top of dirt. When have you ever seen anyone attempt to build anything on dust? What do people normally do with dust? Is it true that dust is generally discarded? Do you know anyone who stores dust as something valuable? Dust is considered worthless.

"So, Mr. Scientist, if you want to copy me, do not begin your experiment with the wrong material. Go, sweep up some dust equal to the size of this pile of dirt, and begin there. I would love to see you make clay out of dust. I would love to see how you will control the dust and make it settle in one place long enough for you to work with it.

"Dirt is heavy; dust is light. Just a little wind will send dust flying in the air. I would like to see what you would mix with dust to make it useful. You can make clay out of dirt, but what in the world are you going to mix with dust to begin your creation?

"You must understand that I took the most worthless material in the universe and formed man. And whether we're talking dust or dirt, I made them both—out of nothing! So you can't compete head-to-head with me unless you first make your building material out of absolutely nothing. There is no way you can do what I do and make what I make because "My glory will I not give to another" (Isaiah 42:8). No one has the blueprints or architectural design to be able to put every muscle, nerve, blood vessel, and system in perfected order and make them work and function with perfect coordination 24/7. My ways are infinitely above your ways."

Thus, the experiment ended abruptly. Where in the world could the scientist find enough dust to begin such an assignment? And what would he do with the dust if he were able to bring it together? The scientist was brought to open shame, for he had no dirt or dust that he could claim to be his own so that he could replicate God's creation.

Of course, I, having majored in biology and minored in chemistry, had some questions of my own. I did not understand how in the world [this scientist was going to make man in a couple of hours,] when it took God a half-day to make the most complex being. Further, it seems to me that the scientist was simply going to sculpt a clay man, which any artist could do. He would form the eyes, nose, ears, lips, etc., and make a clay body. Is man simply a hundred pounds of clay?

How in the world was he going to create this clay-man and afterward put within man all the living systems that God created in us? You have to have a system! The human body is like a complex organization that has an important job to get done on a tight schedule. In order to get everything done perfectly and on time, it has to use a system. Actually, the human body uses many systems that work congruently.

Some of the body's systems are directly connected to the heart, while others are not. Of course, the heart is like the president of the organization. Even if it is not directly involved in the system, it still plays a part. Obviously, if the heart is not working, nothing else is working either. The heart actively participates in the circulatory system, while it just keeps an eye on the respiratory and excretory systems.

If God had allowed the scientist to continue, the man would have had a lot of work to do to create:

- a skeletal system comprised of 206 bones, each of which is made up of many layers of tissue containing blood vessels, nerves, and an inner thick jellylike substance called marrow, which makes blood cells

- a muscular system comprised of more than 700 interactive muscles

- a cardiovascular system which consists of the heart, thousands of vessels, and approximately five liters of blood that these vessels must transport throughout the entire body

- a digestive system which consists of a group of hollow organs working together to convert food into energy and basic nutrients to feed the entire body, and which is capable of ingestion, secretion, mixing, movement, digestion, absorption, and excretion

- a respiratory system which consists of the lungs and its windpipe, with the capacity to oxidize the blood

- an endocrine system which includes all the glands of the body and the hormones produced by those glands, and which is responsible for regulating cellular metabolism, reproduction, sexual development, sugar and mineral homeostasis, heart rate, and digestion

- a reproductive system consisting of several organs which

interact with other systems to give humans the capacity to reproduce

- a nervous system consisting of the brain, spinal cord, sensory organs, and all of the nerves that connect these organs with the rest of the body, and which is responsible for the control of the body and communication among its parts

- immune/lymphatic systems that work to keep harmful agents out of the body, attack those that manage to enter, filter and cleanse the lymph of any debris, abnormal cells, or pathogens, and transport fatty acids from the intestines to the circulatory system

- a urinary system consisting of kidneys, ureters, urinary bladder, and urethra, filters the blood to remove wastes and produce urine

- an integumentary system, which consists of skin, hair, nails, and exocrine glands that protect the body from chemicals, disease, UV light, and physical damage; it also produces sweat, oil, and wax to cool, protect, and moisturize the skin's surface.

Mr. Scientist, please tell me how in the world are you going to create all these systems and place them in the clay man you create? First of all, it seems to me that you are going about this project the wrong way. Besides not having the dust to work with, you are beginning your creation in the wrong order.

It seems to me that you would be wise to use Ezekiel 37 as your guide, where thousands of men were created at the same time. The creation begins with bones, the putting together of the skeletal system. It then adds the muscular system and nervous system and all the other systems of the body. Then God wrapped these systems in human flesh, and, after all this, they were still dead corpses. God had to blow wind and spirit into these corpses to make them live. Are you, Mr. Scientist, capable of doing this after you create your clay man?

Several of our systems are hollow canals. Our respiratory system allows for air to circulate in and out. Our reproductive system allows fluids to flow through its organs. The urinary system allows liquid to pass through it. Our cardiovascular system allows for five liters of blood to flow through it at one time. There are other air spaces within the body to allow greater efficiency of operation of the highly integrated network of human systems.

Mr. Scientist, how are you creating all of this? I could go on and on, speaking of the many layers of tissue and membranes required to make skin, bones, and sensory organs.

The psalmist declares that we are "fearfully and wonderfully" made (Psalm 139:14). It took nothing short of a miracle to make us. We are all miracle babies. No man has God's blueprints on us, and no man will ever be able to duplicate what God has done.

After all, "the earth is the Lord's, and the fullness thereof; the world, and they that dwell therein (Psalm 24:1)." We own nothing, not even a teaspoon of dirt. We manage acres of land and place our names on them as owners, but, the truth be told, we own nothing. GOD OWNS EVERYTHING, and only He knows the purpose for which He created us.

"All things were made by him; and without him was not any thing made that was made" (John 1:3). The Apostle John in Revelation 4:11 expounds on this truth: "Thou art worthy, O Lord, to receive glory and honour and power: for thou hast created all things, and for thy pleasure they are and were created."

Once you understand that the God-ordained life is created by God for His pleasure and for His glory, you should go to the third chapter of Colossians to see how this new you is to function.

VERSE 1:   The God-ordained life is risen with Christ. Therefore, seek those things which are above, where Christ sits on the right hand of God. See yourself as a risen creation. Satan wants to convince you that you are buried beneath a load of care, but always remember your God-ordained position: YOU ARE RISEN!

VERSE 2:   Your affections are on things above, and not on the things of the earth. This makes you a slave and a servant of Jesus Christ exclusively.

VERSE 3:   For your carnal man is dead, and your life is securely hidden with Christ in God. The God-ordained you is dwelling in the secret place of the Most High and abiding under the shadow of the Almighty (Psalm 91:1).

VERSE 4:   When Christ, who is your life, shall appear, you will be with him in glory. Remember: ALL YOUR HOPE IS UP!

VERSE 5:   Therefore, mortify (kill off) the members and properties of your flesh that are upon the earth, namely, fornication, uncleanness, inordinate affection, evil concupiscence, and covetousness, which is idolatry.

VERSE 6:   These properties of the flesh trigger the wrath of God to come upon the children of disobedience.

VERSE 7:   When you are out-of-touch with your God-ordained self, you tend to walk in corruption.

VERSE 8:

But now put off all these, including anger, wrath, malice, blasphemy, filthy communication out of your mouth.

VERSE 9:

Since you have put off the old man with his deeds, you no longer lie one to another.

VERSE 10:

We "have put on the new man [the God-ordained life], which is renewed in knowledge after the image of him that created him."

VERSE 11:

It does not matter what side of the track you were born on; if you are living in the new man, the God-ordained life, Christ is all and in all.

VERSE 12:

Recognize that your God-ordained life is that of the holy and beloved elect of God; therefore, put on bowels of mercies, kindness, humbleness of mind, meekness, long-suffering:

VERSE 13:

Forbear one another (learn to live with or put up with) and forgive one another. When you have heated debates over issues and have very different intellectual, social, and emotional positions regarding them, forgive one another and release it in the name of the Lord, who loved you so much that he forgave you all your sins.

This works in marriages, friendships, and family relations. Do not keep an argument going. State your position distinctly and clearly, and then, at some point, let it go. Do not keep going back and forth, determined to not let the other person have the final say. Once you have made your point clear, you have made your point! LET IT GO!

Now there are some issues that may take several days to resolve. During this time, you weigh each other's positions carefully, discussing the pros and cons of each. Express what you see as a compelling reason and let the facts stand on their own merit. Be civil in your debates. Prolonged heated arguments have the potential of becoming bitter verbal, emotional, and sometimes physical fights.

VERSE 14:   Above all these things, put on love, which is the bond of perfectness.

VERSE 15:   Let the peace of God rule in your heart. This peace is the umpire that calls the shots in your daily communication. This peace will never lead you wrong because it is the peace—the guidance—of God.

VERSE 16:   Let the word of Christ dwell in you richly, enabling you to teach and admonish others in psalms, hymns, and spiritual songs, and to sing with grace in your heart unto the Lord.

VERSE 17:   "And whatever you do in word or deed, do it in the name of the Lord Jesus, giving thanks to God and the Father by him."

VERSES 18-25   Whether you are a wife, a husband, a child, a father, a servant, employee, or employer, or whatever you do, do it heartily as unto the Lord and not unto man. Knowing that it is from the Lord that you will receive the reward of the inheritance, for you serve the Lord Jesus Christ. Be careful with your conduct, because you will receive punishment for the wrong you do, and there is no respect of persons.

When you focus on being a God-ordained person, God will

position you in the world to represent Him in various ways. He will have you at the right place at the right time to meet the right people to do the right thing to get the right results! Our lives will be blessed by God!

When God brought Eve into Adam's life, Adam's God-ordained life expanded to encompass becoming the loving husband for his wife, the caring father and provider for his children, and the master of all living creatures. The God-ordained life is productive and fruitful. He is confidently in charge.

When Adam sinned (depicted in Genesis 3), he lost so much. His God-ordained image was marred and he lost a significant amount of authority and dominion. No longer were all things under his feet. So many things started to happen over which he had no control. The pointing of fingers and blaming others began with sin. Adam lost track of his God-ordained life. Corruption and sin passed on to all the generations following. Now we are faced with violence and evil tragedies that were nonexistent prior to Adam's sin.

The God-ordained life is being the man or the woman that God formed and positioned you to be. God did not make a mistake when He created us. The psalmist puts it this way:

> [13] For Thou hast possessed my reins (my kidneys); Thou hast covered me in my mother's womb. [14] I will praise thee; for I am fearfully and wonderfully made;

marvelous are thy works; and that my soul knowest right well. [15] My substance was not hid from Thee, when I was made in secret, and curiously wrought in the lowest parts of the earth. [16] Thine eyes did see my substance, yet, being unperfect; and in thy book all my members were written, which in continuance were fashioned, when as yet there was none of them. (emphasis mine)

Psalms 139:13–16

Why recreate the wheel when the wheel is already created? Several books support the concept of recreating or reinventing yourself. But why do that when God, who created us, has your "God-ordained you" already made? Take note of the following scripture:

[17] Now the Lord is that spirit: and where the spirit of the Lord is, there is liberty (the freedom to be YOU - God-ordained). [18] But we all, with open face beholding as in a glass (mirror) the glory of the Lord, are changed into the same image from glory to glory, even as by the spirit of the LORD. (emphasis mine)

2 Corinthians 3:17–18

In Adam, we lost track of what God ordained us to be, but in Christ, we regained it. Our God-ordained life is in Christ. "For God, who commanded the light to shine out of darkness, hath shined in our hearts, to give the light of the knowledge of the glory of God in the face of Jesus Christ" (2 Corinthians 4:6).

With joy, let us embrace our new man and the God-ordained life, which will make us able to stand against the wiles of the wicked one and to gain great victories. We are the primary beneficiaries of God's grace and mercy.

> "O Lord, I know that the way of man is not in himself: it is not in man that walks to direct his steps.
>
> Jeremiah 10:23

> Not that we are sufficient of ourselves to think any thing as of ourselves; but our sufficiency is of God.
>
> 2 Corinthians 3:5

> [5] Trust in the Lord with all your heart; and lean not unto your own understanding. [6] In all thy ways, acknowledge him, and he shall direct thy paths.
>
> Proverbs 3:5–6

You are not expected to figure life out by yourself. You are ill-equipped to do so. It is in God that we live, move, and have our being (Acts 17:28). If you want to know the original intent of a machine, go to the manufacturer. He can tell you how it should work. God is our "manufacturer."

> It is he that has made us and not we ourselves; we are his people and the sheep of his pasture.
>
> Psalm 100:3

It was he who created us out of the dust of the ground and breathed into our nostrils the breath of life, and we became a living soul (Genesis 2:7).

Lord, put me in touch with my God-ordained life! My God-ordained life is my spiritually-minded self. "For to be carnally minded is death but to be spiritually minded is life and peace" (Romans 8:6). The God-ordained life always seeks to please GOD and worship and represent the Lord Jesus Christ. Let it be so, Lord!

CHAPTER 5

THE 7 HABITS OF THE GOD-ORDAINED LIFE

Once you understand that the God-ordained life is created by God for His pleasure and for His glory, you are then ready to cultivate the seven habits of a God-ordained life. The first three habits are for personal development. The next are for corporate development. The last habit ties the personal development with the corporate development to make a whole person.

PERSONAL DEVELOPMENT

HABIT 1: HEAR

... O ye dry bones, hear the word of the Lord.

Ezekiel 37:4b

Faith cometh by hearing, and hearing by the word of God.

Romans 10:17

Nothing will happen in the valley of dry bones until God places hearing aids on every bone, giving each bone the capacity to hear. Every bone that will hear the word of the Lord will respond with a motion and get in its proper place.

Hearing causes a reaction! Hearing causes order to come out of chaos. The hearer is more structured, organized, and confident of a brighter future. Hearing creates the platform for faith to stand on.

When the lawyer asks Jesus for the greatest of all commandments, Jesus responds,

> [29] The first of all the commandments is, Hear, O Israel; The Lord our God is one Lord: [30] And thou shalt love the Lord thy God with all thy heart, and with all thy soul, and with all thy mind, and with all thy strength: this is the first commandment.
>
> Mark 12:29–30

Before loving God and loving neighbors, you must hear. So read and quote the word of the Lord aloud so that your ears can hear it and your faith can grow. Each morning, I quote my date-of-birth Psalms and anoint my head with oil. What a blessing it has been to do so!

What is your date of birth? If it is November 7, 1963, you should read and try to commit to memory as much of the 11th, the 7th, and the 63rd Psalms as possible. If your date of birth is May

10, 1983, you should read and try to commit to memory as much of the 5th, the 10th, and the 83rd Psalms as possible. Do you get it? Do this religiously, along with anointing your head with oil, and see what a spiritual energy boost this is.

Faith comes by hearing and hearing by the word of God. Jesus said that the seeds of God's word that fell by the wayside were taken away by the devil from the hearts of the hearers, "lest they should believe and be saved" (Luke 8:12). The word of God will generate faith in your heart, and faith will save you. Thus, Satan acts quickly to steal the word out of the hearers' hearts to prevent them from believing and being saved.

In Luke 22:31–32, Jesus says,

> [21]"Simon, Simon, behold, Satan hath desired to have you, that he may sift you as wheat: [22] But I have prayed for thee, that thy faith fail not: and, when thou are converted, strengthen your brethren."

Hearing will produce faith, and faith will produce salvation. For "this is the victory that overcometh the world, even our faith" (1 John 5:4b).

HABIT 2: BELIEVE

Habit 2 must be developed out of habit 1. Jesus says, "He that believeth on me, as the scripture hath said, out of his belly shall flow rivers of living water" (John 7:38). Faith produces new life and energy. Faith turns the light on in the midst of your dark and troublesome challenges, and the darkness comprehends it not. Faith minimizes the magnitude of your problems and makes all things possible.

In the 9th chapter of Matthew, two blind men follow Jesus, crying, "Thou Son of David, have mercy on us." Jesus does not respond immediately, but continues on his journey and goes into a house. These blind men follow Him all the way into the house. They cannot see, so they probably stumble and fall along the way, but they do not let a stumble or fall prevent them from following the noise of the crowd and getting to Jesus. They enter the house where Jesus is and continue to cry for mercy. Jesus finally answers them, "Believe ye that I am able to do this?"

And they respond, "Yea, Lord." Jesus then touches their eyes and says unto them, "According to your faith be it unto you."

In the gospel according to Luke, the woman who has the issue of blood—a continuous flow that would not stop, making her weaker and weaker day by day—comes to Jesus amid a crowd. So she presses her way through the crowd, saying to herself, if I can just touch the hem of his garment, I know I will be made whole. She touches his garment, and immediately the fountain of her blood dries up. She is healed of her plague.

Jesus looks around and asks, "Who touched my clothes?" The

disciples respond with grave concern. "Master, with so many people crowding around trying to touch You, You ask who touched You?" Jesus looks around, knowing that virtue had gone out of him. He repeats, "Somebody touched me." When he catches the eye of the woman who has been healed, she falls down at his feet and tells her story. Jesus says to her, "Daughter . . . thy faith hath made thee whole; go in peace" (Luke 8:45–48).

In the 9th chapter of Mark, a worried father brings to Jesus his son who has a dumb spirit that is destroying the child, oftentimes throwing the child into the fire and into the water. He says to Jesus, I brought my child to your disciples for them to cast this spirit out, but they could not. "But if thou canst do any thing, have compassion on us, and help us" (Mark 9:22).

Jesus answers him, "If thou canst believe, all things are possible to him that believeth." The father immediately cries out, "Lord, I believe; help thou mine unbelief." Jesus then rebukes the foul spirit, saying, "Thou dumb and deaf spirit, I charge thee, come out of him, and enter no more into him." The evil spirit leaves the child seemingly dead, but Jesus lifts the child up from the ground and presents a delivered child to the father. The disciples afterward ask Jesus why they were not able to deliver the child. And Jesus says to them, "This kind can come forth by nothing, but by prayer and fasting" (Mark 9:23–25, 28–29).

At some point you need to ask yourself, "How badly do you want to see your loved ones delivered? Are you willing to make the sacrifice to make this happen? If Jesus said that prayer and fasting will empower you to work miracles, why are you not giving yourself to prayer and fasting?"

Why not start a new habit? Choose any 24-hour period once per week and fast. Even people who take medicine daily can do this without interrupting the scheduled intake of medicine. (WARNING! When you take medicine, you must eat! You cannot take medicine on an empty stomach. I will see you in ER!)

So, you choose the 24-hour period. From nine a.m. today to nine a.m. tomorrow is twenty-four hours. Thus, you are able to take your medication after eating a hearty breakfast, and then eat no more for twenty-four hours. That is a 24-hour fast. You do not have to be cheated out of an opportunity to pray and fast. Where there is a will, there is a way.

This may work well for people who exert much physical energy while working. The breakfast in the morning will give strength for the day, leaving you hungry later; but you should expect to suffer some when you fast because the flesh is being crucified. So you pray and go to bed, then eat the next morning (after twenty-four hours), giving you strength for that day.

Please understand that I use this simply as an example of a 24-hour period. Whether it is from nine a.m. to nine a.m. the next day, from nine p.m. to nine p.m. the next night, or from noon to noon the next day, or some other time period, you choose the 24-hour period, and fast every week for the next 52 weeks. Watch God do wonders!

Daniel 11:32 reads, "The people that do know their God shall be strong, and do exploits." They shall be strong and do exploits at a time when wickedness is prevailing throughout the earth and a deceiving spirit is corrupting those who profess faith in God but do not intimately know God. This prevailing spirit will not diminish the power of God in the lives of His people. They shall be strong and do exploits! So have faith in God! For this faith will always lead to victory.

One Sunday I preached on faith and hoping to the end! Do not give up! Believe God! In preparation for the sermon, I got to church before service time to extend a long, heavy string around the outside of the sanctuary, with the beginning of the string on the pulpit. At the climax of my sermon, I asked for a volunteer to come and begin pulling on this string.

A sister ran down out of the choir stand and began to pull on the string. While she was pulling, I was driving home the need to be consistent and persistent in our endeavors to get our prayers answered.

I looked at the sister and said, "You have been pulling on that string for more than five minutes and all you are getting is more string. You know the definition of insanity, so why are you continuing to pull on a string that is getting you nothing?" She replied, "You told me to pull on the string, and until you tell me to stop, I am going to pull on this string."

I turned to the congregants and asked whether she should continue pulling on this string. They encouraged her to keep pulling on the string. So, she continued pulling on the string while I continued with my sermon.

As I approached the close of my sermon, I looked at the dear sister and said, "What good is faith, if, after you believe and believe and believe, you still come up empty? You have been pulling on this string for almost fifteen minutes, and all you have at your feet are yards and yards of string. Are you ready to walk away?"

She replied, "No, because I feel a resistance on this string. I think I have got something." So, she pulled faster and faster, and finally the end of that string was in her hand. At the end of that string, I had attached a one-hundred-dollar bill. Her reward for not giving up was one hundred dollars for fifteen minutes of looking foolish in front of hundreds of people and believing God for something that had no sign of coming.

You can imagine that she left the pulpit rejoicing. It pays to do the same thing over and over when you know that you are doing the right thing. For according to the author of Hebrews 11:1, "Faith is the substance of things hoped for, the evidence of things not seen." As long as she simply continued pulling on the string, which had a hundred-dollar bill attached to it, she was sure to get a blessing. And that is another sermon: "Keep Pulling the String!"

HABIT 3: PRAY

In the 11th chapter of Mark, Jesus curses a fig tree because he looks for fruit on it and finds none. The tree quickly withers away, causing Peter to remark with amazement, "Master, behold, the fig tree which thou cursedst is withered away." Jesus says to his disciples, "Have faith in God." If you believe the things that you say, you shall have whatever you say. "Therefore I say unto you, What things soever ye desire, when you pray, believe that ye receive them, and you shall have them" (Mark 11:12–22, 24).

In the 6th Chapter of 2 Chronicles, Solomon intercedes on behalf of the people of Israel. He entreats God to hear, deliver and answer the prayers of the people when, because of their own folly, they fall into sin and suffer the consequences of it. Solomon begs for God's forgiveness and His mercy.

In the 7th Chapter of 2 Chronicles, Solomon makes sacrifices unto the Lord and conducts a solemn assembly – 7 days of feasting – and sends the people home rejoicing.

> [12] And the Lord appeared to Solomon by night, and said unto him, I have heard thy prayer, and have chosen this place to myself for an house of sacrifice.[13] If I shut up heaven that there be no rain, or if I command the locusts to devour the land, or it I send pestilence among my people; [14] If my people, which are called by my

name, shall humble themselves, and pray, and seek my face, and turn from their wicked ways; then will I hear from heaven, and will forgive their sin, and will heal their land. [15]Now mine eyes shall be open, and mine ears attend unto the prayer that is made in this place.

2 Chronicles 7:12-15

[1]Bless the Lord, O my soul: and all that is within me, bless his holy name. [2]Bless the Lord, O my soul, and forget not all his benefits: [3]Who forgiveth all thine iniquities; who healeth all thy diseases; [4]Who redeemeth thy life from destruction; who crowneth thee with lovingkindness and tender mercies; [5]Who satisfieth thy mouth with good things; so that thy youth is renewed like the eagle's.

Psalm 103:1-5

"What a friend we have in Jesus, all our sins and griefs to bear. What a privilege to carry everything to God in prayer. Oh, what peace we often forfeit. Oh, what needless pain we bear. All because we do not carry everything to God in prayer!" This is a hymn originally written by Joseph M. Scriven to comfort his mother, who was living in Ireland while he was in Canada.

I have difficulty singing the song "Not my father nor my mother, but it's me, O Lord, standing in the need of prayer. Not my sister nor my brother, but it's me, O Lord, standing in the need of prayer." I have a problem with that song because my father, my mother, my sister, and my brother all need the Lord, and we all are standing in the need of prayer. My praying must be inclusive not exclusive.

Jesus teaches his disciples to pray after this manner: "Our Father which art in heaven, Hallowed be thy name ..." (Matthew 6:9 and Luke 11:2). Not "My Father" but "Our Father!" We must not be selfish in our praying. 1 Timothy 2:1–4 reads as follows:

> [1]I exhort therefore, that, first of all, supplications, prayers, intercessions, and giving of thanks, be made for all men; [2] For kings, and for all that are in authority; that we may lead a quiet and peaceable life in all godliness and honesty. [3] For this is good and acceptable in the sight of God our Saviour; [4] Who will have all men to be saved, and to come unto the knowledge of the truth.

According to the Gospel of St. Luke, Jesus speaks a parable that concludes that men ought always to pray, and not to faint. There was in a city a judge who did not fear God, neither regarded man. In the same city there was a widow who was being pestered by an adversary, who was of course making her life miserable. So, she appealed to the judge, who could—if he willed—put a stop to the threatening actions of her adversary.

The widow did not let the reputation of the unjust judge prevent her from pursuing relief from him. Neither did she allow his ignoring her to discourage her. She continued day after day making her request known to the judge.

I have been through both management and leadership training and have heard over and over again that the definition of insanity is doing the same thing over and over again, while expecting different results. "If you keep doing the same thing over and over again, you will get the same results," presenters have emphasized. Thank God, this widow did not go to those seminars and conferences! She would have missed her blessing. She continued day after day doing the same thing, expecting different results.

My experience in the chemistry lab at UIC proved that there was an exception to this dogma taught to supervisors and administrators. I placed in a beaker a few milliliters of a clear liquid base called sodium hydroxide (NaOH), commonly known as lye. It was my assignment to determine how many milliliters of the clear liquid hydrochloric acid (HCl) it would take to turn this clear liquid base (NaOH) in the beaker into a blue solution. Since I did not have a clue how soon the HCl would turn the clear base to blue, I controlled the speed of the drip.

After waiting and watching several minutes with the HCl continuously dripping and getting not even a hint of a color change, I thought maybe the professor was playing an April Fool's joke on us. It seemed that no change was coming any time soon. So I became impatient and started pouring, not dripping, the liquid HCl acid into the NaOH. Suddenly I saw a streak of color. That was an indication that I was getting close to the change I was looking for. Still impatient, I poured more HCl into the beaker of NaOH, and the entire beaker turned blue.

At that point, I knew then that I had destroyed my experiment because I could not determine the drop that made the difference. I knew then that I would have to start over.

But, when I stirred the base solution in the beaker, it turned clear again. Thank God, my experiment was not lost! You had better believe that I was extremely cautious from that point forward.

So, I wiped my forehead in relief and began very slowly dripping the HCl into the NaOH solution until the base liquid turned blue. I was able to record my results and get a good score for that assignment. But I had to keep doing the same thing over and over again until change came.

The fifth chapter of Luke holds a wonderful story of doing the same thing over and over until change comes. In it, we see Peter, a fisherman who is sorely disappointed at being unable to catch any fish the night before. "We have toiled all the night, and have taken nothing, (Luke 5:5)" Peter laments to Jesus after Jesus tells him to "launch out into the deep, and let down your nets for a draught" (Luke 5:4). Peter humbly obeys, "At thy word I will let down the net" (Luke 5:5). In other words, "We have failed all night, but, if you say so, we will try it again. The timing seems bad. Based on my experience, you do not fish in the morning when the sun is shining.

But, if you say so, we will do what you say do."

When Peter does what Jesus commands, he catches more fish than his net can hold, all because he did the same thing over and over again, expecting a different result. The blessing did come to the sister who kept pulling the string. The sodium hydroxide base did turn from clear to blue when I continued pouring into it hydrogen chloride. The unjust judge did grant the widow what she requested. He says,

> [4] Though I fear not God, nor regard man; [5] yet because this widow troubleth me, I will avenge her, lest by her continual coming she weary me. [6] And the Lord said, Hear what the unjust judge saith. [7] And shall not God avenge his own elect, which cry day and night unto him, though he bear long with them? [8] I tell you that he will avenge them speedily. Nevertheless when the Son of man cometh, shall he find faith on the earth?
>
> Luke 18:4–8

JUST KEEP ON PRAYING, FOR THE LORD IS NIGH. JUST KEEP ON PRAYING. HE WILL HEAR YOUR CRY. FOR THE LORD HAS PROMISED, AND HIS WORD IS TRUE. JUST KEEP ON PRAYING. HE'LL ANSWER YOU!

(Saints Don't Stop Praying, Lyrics by G.E. Patterson)

CORPORATE DEVELOPMENT

HABIT 4: LOVE

Whatever you do for others on the horizontal level should flow out of your love for God on the vertical level. This is the reason Jesus tells the scribe in Mark 12:28–31 to love God first, then love his neighbor. You must establish an intimate relationship with God before having a meaningful and lasting relationship with others.

We love God because He first loved us and gave unto us His only begotten Son, Jesus, so that we, believing in Jesus, will not perish but have everlasting life. "God sent not his Son into the world to condemn the world; but that the world through him might be saved" (John 3:16–17).

So, this is how it is: God loved us so much that he gave to us His Son. Jesus loved us so much that He gave us (sacrificed) His life by shedding his blood by the way of the cross to save us from our sins. God invested all of himself in Jesus so that in Jesus would dwell "all the fullness of the Godhead bodily" (Colossians 2:9).

Jesus tells Thomas in the 14th chapter of St. John that when you see Him, you see the Father, because He and the Father are one. Jesus had already given them words of comfort when he said, "Let not your heart be troubled: ye believe in God, believe also in me" (John 14:1).

In the 6th chapter of St. John, some people come to Jesus and ask him, "What shall we do, that we might work the works of God?" Jesus replies, "This is the work of God, that ye believe on Him whom He hath sent" (John 6:28–29).

In the 5th chapter of St. John, Jesus responds to the Jews who have accused Him of making Himself equal with God:

> [19] Verily, Verily, I say unto you, The Son can do nothing of himself, but what he seeth the Father do: for what things soever he doeth, these also doeth the Son likewise. [20] For the Father loveth the Son, and showeth him all things that himself doeth: and he will shew him greater works than these, that ye may marvel. [21] For as the Father raiseth up the dead, and quickeneth them; even so the Son quickeneth whom he will. [22] For the Father judgeth no man, but hath committed all judgment unto the Son: [23] That all men should honour the Son, even as they honour the Father. He that honoureth not the Son honoureth not the Father which hath sent him. [24] Verily, verily, I say unto you, He that heareth my word, and believeth on him that sent me, hath everlasting life, and shall not come into condemnation; but is passed from death unto life
>
> .   John 5:19–24

Everyone must love and honor the one whom God has sent to save us and bless us.

The Hawkins family recorded a song more than forty years ago that says,

"Dear JESUS, I love you
You're a Friend of mine.
You supply my every need;
my hungry soul you feed.
I'm aware you are my source,
from whom all blessings flow.
And, with this thought in mind,
I know just where to go."

Every week, before I begin my sermon, I open with the following prayer:

"Dear Jesus, we love You, we praise You, we honour and adore You, we extol You and esteem You infinitely above all others, because You are God. There is none like You in all the earth. For it is You who have made us and not we ourselves. We are your people and the sheep of your pasture. So, we enter into your gates with thanksgiving and into your courts with praise. We thank You and bless your name because You are so good. Your mercy is everlasting, and your truth endures to all generations. And we just want to say THANK YOU, THANK YOU, THANK YOU, THANK YOU, THANK YOU!"

Why not take a little time right now and thank the Lord for his kindness toward you? Take time to say, "I thank you for your goodness, Lord. Yes, I do. I thank you for your mercy, for how you brought me through. I thank you for your saving grace; there is no one who can take your place. I thank you for your goodness, Lord. Yes, I do." Thank him, for "he was wounded for our transgressions, he was bruised for our iniquities: the chastisement of our peace was upon him; and with his stripes we are healed" Isaiah 53:5. Go ahead and thank him!

Jesus says that our love is measured by our obedience to him. "Why call ye me, Lord, Lord, and do not the things which I say?" (Luke 6:46). "If ye love me, keep my commandments" (John 14:15). Love is measured by obedience! Let us seek to do His will and to finish His work.

Jesus further insists on self-denial as recorded in two of the four Gospels: "If any man will come after me, let him deny himself, and take up his cross daily, and follow me" (Matthew 16:24; Luke 9:23). Self-denial is prerequisite to loving Jesus.

As recorded in John 21:15–17, Jesus approaches Peter on the seashore of Galilee, after Peter had caught a net full of fish, and asks him three questions:

1. "Simon Peter . . . lovest thou me more than these?"

2. "Simon, lovest thou me?"

3. "Simon, lovest thou me?"

Each time, Peter answers, "Yea, Lord; thou knowest that I love thee" (John 21:16). Jesus then challenges Peter to feed his lambs and his sheep. Jesus, in essence, is saying that we must look beyond our own wants and cravings to move forward His agenda, which is to save the lost, preach the good news to the poor, heal the brokenhearted, deliver the captives, give sight to the blind, and set at liberty them that are bruised. We must show our love to Jesus by faithful duty to Him.

Loving God is the first commandment. Loving our neighbor as ourselves is the second commandment. In both cases, self-denial and self-sacrifice are required. Remember, love is an action word!

So, the question is raised in the Gospel according to St. Luke, "Who is my neighbor?" Jesus explains with a story about a man who, while traveling from Jerusalem to Jericho, was attacked by thieves. The thieves beat him, striped him, and left him half-dead. Both a priest and a Levite not only passed the wounded man but even crossed over to the other side so that they would not have any contact with him (Luke 10:29–32).

But a Samaritan who was passing by had compassion on the man. He poured oil and wine onto the traveler's wound, bound it up, placed him on his own beast, carried the man into town, and found an inn. There he cared for the wounded man. He did not just drop him off, but he stayed overnight with this man to ensure that he began to recover (Luke 10:33–34).

Upon leaving the inn, the Samaritan pulled out money, gave it to the host, and said, "Take care of him; and whatsoever thou spendest more, when I come again, I will repay thee" (Luke 10:35). In other words, whatever you do, take care of him!

Jesus then asks the lawyer who wants to know who his neighbor is, "Which now of these three, thinkest thou, was neighbour unto him that fell among the thieves?" The lawyer answers, "He that shewed mercy on him." Jesus further encourages to him, "Go, and do thou likewise" (Luke 10:36-37)!

If you are going to love your neighbor as yourself, you must pull aside the drapery, lift up the shade, raise the window, stick your big head out of the window, and see someone else who is in need beside yourself!

Jesus, in preparing his disciples for his departure, says in John 13:34–35:

> [34] A new commandment I give unto you, That ye love one another; as I have loved you, that you also love one another. [35] By this shall all men know that ye are my disciples, if ye have love one to another."

Jesus makes it clear that the one criterion that will determine whether we are his disciples is how much we love and care for each other. The world will recognize us, not by our dance or our shout, but by how well we take care of each other.

Lord, help us to major in the majors and minor in the minors. Everything else may be good and admirable, but the one thing that matters most is how much we love God and how much we love each other.

Apostle John in 1 John 4:7–21 expounds further:

> 7 Beloved, let us love one another: for love is of God; and every one that loveth is born of God, and knoweth God. 8 He that loveth not knoweth not God; for God is love. 9 In this was manifested the love of God toward us, because that God sent his only begotten Son into the world, that we might live through him. 10 Herein is love, not that we loved God, but that he loved us, and sent his Son to be the propitiation for our sins. 11 Beloved, if God so loved us, we ought also to love one another. 12 No man hath seen God at any time. If we love one another, God dwelleth in us, and his love is perfected in us. 13 Hereby know we that we dwell in him, and he in us, because he hath given us of his Spirit. 14 And we have seen and do testify that the Father sent the Son to be the Saviour of the world. 15 Whosoever shall confess that Jesus is the Son of God, God dwelleth in him, and he in God. 16 And we have known and believed the love that God hath to us. God is love; and he that dwelleth in love dwelleth in God, and God in him.

[17] Herein is our love made perfect, that we may have boldness in the day of judgment: because as he is, so are we in this world. [18] There is no fear in love; but perfect love casteth out fear: because fear hath torment. He that feareth is not made perfect in love. [19] We love him, because he first loved us. [20] If a man say, I love God, and hateth his brother, he is a liar: for he that loveth not his brother whom he hath seen, how can he love God whom he hath not seen? [21] And this commandment have we from him, That he who loveth God love his brother also.

Love God and love one another!

HABIT 5: WORK

In the book of St. John, Jesus exclaims,

> I must work the works of him that sent me, while it is day: the night cometh, when no man can work.
>
> John 9:4

> My meat is to do the will of him that sent me, and to finish his work.
>
> John 4:34

[12] Verily, verily, I say unto you, He that believeth on me, the works that I do shall he do also; and greater works than these shall he do; because I go unto my

Father. [13] And whatsoever ye shall ask in my name, that will I do, that the Father may be glorified in the Son. [14] If ye shall ask any thing in my name, I will do it.

John 14:12–14

WHAT A PROMISE! The Lord has given us so much to work with. Let us get busy doing the will of the Lord and moving His agenda forward.

The Apostle James picks it up in his book by saying:

[14] What doth it profit, my brethren, though a man say he has faith, and have not works? can faith save him? [15] If a brother or sister be naked, and destitute of daily food, [16] And one of you say unto them, Depart in peace, be ye warmed and filled; notwithstanding ye give them not those things which are needful to the body; what doth it profit? [17] Even so faith, if it hath not works, is dead, being alone. [18] Yea, a man may say, Thou hast faith, and I have works: shew me thy faith without thy works, and I will shew thee my faith by my works. [19] Thou believest that there is one God; thou doest well: the devils also believe, and tremble. [20] But wilt thou know, O vain man, that faith without works is dead? [21] Was not Abraham our father justified by works, when he had offered Isaac his son upon

the altar? [22] Seest thou how faith wrought with his works, and by works was faith made perfect? [23] And the scripture was fulfilled which saith, Abraham believed God, and it was imputed unto him for righteousness: and he was called the Friend of God. [24] Ye see then how that by works a man is justified, and not by faith only. [25] Likewise also did works justify not Rahab the harlot, when she had received the messengers, and had sent them out another way? [26] For as the body without the spirit is dead, so faith without works is dead also.

James 2:14–26

Paul says to the saints in Ephesus, "We are his workmanship, created in Christ Jesus unto good works, which God has before ordained that we should walk in them" (Ephesians 2:10). He further says to Titus, "[Jesus] gave himself for us, that he might redeem us from all iniquity, and purify unto himself a peculiar people, zealous of good works" (Titus 2:14).

In the Beatitudes, Jesus teaches his disciples to, "Let your light so shine before men, that they may see your good works, and glorify your Father which is in heaven" (Matthew 5:16).

What are the good works you have been called to do? They are deeds done to and for people to meet their needs and heal their hurts. More specifically, you are to do the works of Jesus as found in Luke 4:18–19; Matthew 25:35–36; Luke 19:10; 1 Thessalonians

5:14; James 5:16; 1 Corinthians 14:12; and Jude 20. They are:

- preach the gospel to the poor

- heal the brokenhearted

- preach deliverance to the captives

- preach recovering of sight to the blind

- set at liberty them that are bruised

- preach the acceptable year of the Lord

- feed the hungry

- give drink to the thirsty

- house the homeless

- clothe the naked

- visit the sick

- give personal attention to the incarcerated

- seek and save the lost

- warn the unruly

- comfort the feebleminded

- support the weak

- be patient toward all men

- confess your faults one to another and pray one for another that ye may be healed

- seek that you may excel to the edifying of the church

- build up yourself on your most holy faith, praying in the Holy Ghost

There is much work to do. So find yourself working on this list every day. "To do good and to communicate forget not: for with such sacrifices God is well pleased" (Hebrews 13:16).

> [20] Now the God of peace, that brought again from the dead our Lord Jesus, that great shepherd of the sheep, through the blood of the everlasting covenant, [21] Make you perfect in every good work to do his will, working in you that which is well pleasing in his sight, through Jesus Christ; to whom be glory for ever and ever. Amen.
>
> Hebrews 13:20–21

HABIT 6: FELLOWSHIP

> [16] Then they that feared the Lord spake often one to another: and the Lord hearkened, and heard it, and a book of remembrance was written before him

for them that feared the Lord, and that thought upon his name. [17] And they shall be mine, saith the Lord of hosts, in that day when I make up my jewels; and I will spare them, as a man spareth his own son that serves him.

Malachi 3:16–17

The members of the church must come out of their closets and spend time together, "not forsaking the assembling of [yourselves] together" (Hebrews 10:25). There is much to be gained by fellowship. Shortly after Pentecost, the spirit-filled believers went from house to house, breaking bread and eating their meat with "gladness and singleness of heart," according to Acts 2:46. They were "praising God, and having favour with all the people. And the Lord added to the church daily such as should be saved" (Acts 2:47).

The word fellowship means to share in common; to communicate; to be joined together in a common union; to be united spiritually, socially, and emotionally. It causes people to interact with each other because they feel and sense a common bond. First Corinthians 12:13 reads, "For by one spirit are we all baptized into one body, whether we be Jews or Gentiles, whether we be bond or free; and have been all made to drink into one spirit."

The Apostle Paul goes on to tell the church at Corinth that

we are many members but one body, and that God has placed the members in the body where He wanted them. He has given each of them abundant honor, so that there would be "no schism in the body; but that the members should have the same care one for another" (1 Corinthians 12:25).

First John 1:5–7 says:

> [5] This then is the message which we have heard of him, and declare unto you, that God is light, and in him is no darkness at all. [6] If we say that we have fellowship with him, and walk in darkness, we lie, and do not the truth: [7] But if we walk in the light, as he is in the light, we have fellowship one with another, and the blood of Jesus Christ his Son cleanses us from all sin."

Let us make sure that we guard our tongue and guide our bodies so that we do nothing to break fellowship with God or with each other. James 3:2 reads, "For in many things we offend all. If any man offend not in word, the same is a perfect man, and able also to bridle the whole body."

James further says in verses 13–18 of chapter 3:

> [13] Who is a wise man and endued with knowledge among you? let him show out of a good conversation his works with meekness of wisdom. [14] But if you have bitter envying and strife in your

hearts, glory not, and lie not against the truth. [15] This wisdom descends not from above, but is earthly, sensual, devilish. [16] For where envying and strife is, there is confusion and every evil work. [17] But the wisdom that is from above is first pure, then peaceable, gentle, and easy to be intreated, full of mercy and good fruits, without partiality, and without hypocrisy. [18] And the fruit of righteousness is sown in peace of them that make peace."

As Paul encourages the saints in Ephesus, let us "[endeavor] to keep the unity of the Spirit in the bond of peace" (Ephesians 4:3), for we are in the body of Christ together. Learn how to "comprehend with all saints" (Ephesians 3:18). Relax and get to know them who labor among us. For WE ARE BETTER TOGETHER!

HABIT 7: WORSHIP

Now let us wrap all the other six habits in the blanket of WORSHIP. God said to Isaiah that he would give to us "beauty for ashes, the oil of joy for mourning, and the garment of praise for the spirit of heaviness; that they might be called trees of righteousness, the planting of the Lord, that he might be glorified" (Isaiah 61:3). Worship brings glory to God! It focuses on Him.

Jesus says to the Samaritan woman at the well, "But the hour cometh, and now is, when the true worshippers shall worship the

Father in spirit and in truth: for the Father seeketh such to worship him" (St. John 4:23). The Father is looking for true worshippers, for they are closest to His heart.

To understand better the meaning of worship (since it is not defined in scripture), I took note of the first time the word is used in scripture. Worship appears for the first time in Genesis 22:5, when Abraham is preparing to offer to God the most prized possession of his life, his son Isaac. From this we see that worship is connected to the sacrifice of something that we value.

In Romans 12:1–2, Paul shows us that the sacrifice of our own bodies is to be part of our worship.

> [1] I beseech you therefore, brethren, by the mercies of God, that ye present your bodies a living sacrifice, holy, acceptable unto God, which is your reasonable service. [2] And be not conformed to this world; but be ye transformed by the renewing of your mind, that ye might prove what is that good, and acceptable, and perfect, will of God.

Our bodies are our most precious earthly gift. Satan somehow had convinced himself that if God would allow him to touch Job's body, Job would curse God. Satan knew that Job, like all of us, valued his life. But Job was too committed to God to allow prolonged illness to cause him to curse God or charge God foolishly. Instead, Job worshiped God, saying, "The Lord gave, and the Lord hath taken away; blessed be the name of the Lord" (Job 1:21). Satan was not able to defeat Job's faith and trust in God. So bless the Lord at all times, and let his praises be continually in your mouth (Psalm 34:1).

In 1 Chronicles 16:8–31, David delivers to his chief director of music, Asaph, and to his brethren the following Psalm:

> [8] Give thanks unto the Lord, call upon his name, make known his deeds among the people. [9] Sing unto him, sing psalms unto him, talk ye of all his wondrous works. [10] Glory ye in his holy name: let the heart of them rejoice that seek the Lord. [11] Seek the Lord and his strength, seek his face continually. [12] Remember his marvellous works that he hath done, his wonders, and the judgments of his mouth; [13] O ye seed of Israel his servant, ye children of Jacob, his chosen ones. [14] He is the Lord our GOD; his judgments are in all the earth. [15] Be ye mindful always of his covenant; the word which he commanded to a thousand generations; [16] Even of the covenant which he made with Abraham, and of his oath unto Isaac; [17] And hath confirmed the same to Jacob for a law, and to Israel for an everlasting covenant, [18] Saying, Unto thee will I give the land of Canaan, the lot of your inheritance; [19] When ye were but few, even a few, and strangers in it. [20] And when they went from nation to nation, and from

one kingdom to another people; [21] He suffered no man to do them wrong: yea, he reproved kings for their sakes, [22] Saying, Touch not mine anointed, and do my prophets no harm. [23] Sing unto the Lord, all the earth; shew forth from day to day his salvation. [24] Declare his glory among the heathen; his marvellous works among all nations. [25] For great is the Lord, and greatly to be praised: he also is to be feared above all gods. [26] For all the gods of the people are idols: but the Lord made the heavens. [27] Glory and honour are in his presence; strength and gladness are in his place. [28] Give unto the Lord, ye kindreds of the people, give unto the Lord glory and strength. [29] Give unto the Lord the glory due unto his name: bring an offering, and come before him: worship the Lord in the beauty of holiness. [30] Fear before him, all the earth: the world also shall be stable, that it be not moved. [31] Let the heavens be glad, and let the earth rejoice: and let men say among the nations, the Lord reigneth.

When you worship, you submit your will to Him; the focus is on Him. The sacrifice of your lips, the sacrifice of your substance, and the sacrifice of yourself are all a part of worship. Every day, this must be the habit of the God-ordained life. May God bless you as you cultivate the seven habits of a God-ordained life!

CHAPTER 6
LESSONS FROM THE HAND

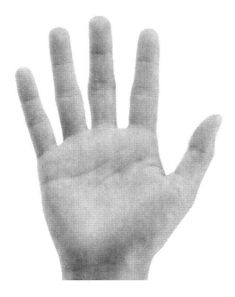

Imagine a normal hand with a thumb and four fingers. The third finger is like the center of a basketball team. The second and fourth fingers are like forwards, and the baby finger and thumb are like guards. Each finger is different from the other, and the thumb stands out as very odd and different. While all these fingers share a common palm, each has a unique assignment.

The fingers and the thumb take on specific assignments based on their position in relation to the palm. Think of the palm as the common qualifications that all God-ordained persons must have. In other words, the palm can represent God's standard of holiness and principles of righteousness. Psalm 48:10b reads, "Thy right hand is full of righteousness." This means that He is a covenant-keeper in redemption. What He has promised, He will perform. This word righteousness also means complete and total deliverance, and decisive victory. It further includes prosperity in the future. Simply put, His right hand is full of what is so, or what ought to be so.

Thus, His right hand fixes whatever needs to be fixed and justifies whatever needs correction. According to Psalm 98:1, His right hand and holy arm has gotten him the victory. So, understand how powerful this reality is: we are members of His right hand. GOD uses us to make things right on the earth. We are the salt of the earth and the light of the world (Matthew 5:13–14). Everything that we need to function effectively is in His hand. All believers, as members of the palm, are expected to work together, never *against* each other, but *for* each other. Likewise, we are to serve one another and provoke one another unto love and good works (Hebrews 10:24).

Jesus declared that men would glorify God when they see our good works (St. Matthew 5:16). Paul says to Titus that Jesus "gave himself for us, that he might redeem us from all iniquity, and purify unto himself a peculiar people, zealous of good works" (Titus 2:14).

All of our good works can be summed up in one word: love. Jesus reminds his disciples:

> [34] A new commandment I give unto you, That ye love one another; as I have loved you, that ye also love one another. [35] By this shall all men know that ye are my disciples, if you have love one to another.
>
> John 13:34–35

We must welcome every opportunity presented to us to show love and good works to each other and to the people of our community and world.

Most of what I have shared with you thus far is the common ground we all share in Christ. It is the foundation of what all God-ordained persons should be. As we grow in grace and in the knowledge of our Lord Jesus Christ, we are given specific assignments that are uniquely ours. We must accept these assignments and not be ashamed to go forward and operate in our gifts.

Everyone attached to the Lord's hand must be filled with the Spirit and possess the fruit of the Spirit. But not everyone has the same gift or gifts as other members of the palm. The Lord gives spiritual gifts individually as He will. Everybody gets a gift! There is no reason for anyone in the body of Christ to stand idly by, bored, with nothing to do. We read in 1 Corinthians 12:11 that everybody gets a gift! Remember "we are his workmanship, created in Christ

Jesus unto good works" (Ephesians 2:10).

Now, it is up to you how effectively you use the gift or gifts He gives you. You will have to answer to God regarding your effective or ineffective use of His gift. His gift will work if you use it. It was given to you to edify the body of Christ. It will work, if you work it!

Come before the throne of grace in daily prayer and seek to know the will of God for your life. He will reveal it to you. He might send a confirmation through another servant of the Lord. You will know it is the Lord because this person will speak into your life the very things you had been pondering. Get busy preparing yourself to be an effective servant of the Lord.

The 12th chapter of 1 Corinthians lists spiritual gift. You possess one of these, maybe two or three. Which gift is it for you?

Spiritual gifts do three things: 1) exalt Jesus Christ as Lord; 2) edify, build, and unite the church of Jesus Christ; and 3) bring profit to the operators of the gifts. This ensures that there will be no schisms or divisions in the body of Christ and that the members should have the same care one for another. "And whether one member suffer, all the members suffer with it; or one member be honoured, all the members rejoice with it" (1 Corinthians 12:26).

There are diversities of gifts, differences of administrations, and diversities of operations, but the same spirit, the same Lord, and the same God who works and operates in all (1 Corinthians

12:4–6). Here are the gifts as referenced in 1 Corinthians 12:8–10:

1. the word of wisdom – a sense of direction or an unction of what the next step should be

2. the word of knowledge – an awareness of people, elements, or events not yet manifested

3. faith – an unshakeable belief in God despite all odds, so that absolutely nothing makes you doubt God

4. gifts of healing – an ability to cause sicknesses, infirmities, illnesses, and discomforts to move out of the body when you pray

5. working of miracles – an ability to perform that which is humanly and scientifically impossible

6. prophecy – an ability to tell not only what is going to happen in the future but also what to do about it

7. discernment of spirits – an ability to distinguish the spirit of truth from the spirit of error

8. divers kinds of tongues – an ability to speak in various languages that you have not been taught

9. interpretation of tongues – an ability to understand and interpret messages spoken in various unknown tongues, for the purpose of edifying the church

And God has set some in the church as referenced in 1 Corinthians 12:28:

1. apostles – sent to establish churches in various places and

organize the leadership of them

2. prophets – preachers or proclaimers of the gospel

3. teachers – instructors who give understanding of the scriptures

4. miracles – performing that which is humanly and scientifically impossible

5. gifts of healing – moving sicknesses, illnesses, discomforts, evil spirits out of the body

6. helps – sense of order; willing and ready to assist; volunteers to extend hand

7. governments – administration: a sense of how all parts work together

8. diversities of tongues – various languages

Even more important than your gift is the driving force that causes you to us it. Unless you operate your gift based on your love for God and your love for others, it is useless. Paul says that if, after all the manifestations of your gifts, you do not have love, you are as "sounding brass" (1 Corinthians 13:1). You are nothing, and all that you do profits you nothing. In order to bring glory to God, you must have love. As it is referenced in 1 Corinthians 13:4–8, love:

1. suffers long

2. is kind

3. envies not

4. vaunts not itself

5. is not puffed up

6. does not behave itself unseemly

7. seeks not her own

8. is not easily provoked

9. thinks no evil

10. rejoices not in iniquity

11. rejoices in truth

12. bears all things

13. believes all things

14. hopes all things

15. endures all things

16. never fails

"And now abideth faith, hope, and love, these three; but the greatest of these is love" (1 Corinthians 13:13). So "follow after love, and desire spiritual gifts" (1 Corinthians 14:1).

Did you identify your gift? Do you see your spiritual niche? Start with love, and let God dictate the rest to you. We, the family of God and the body of Christ, need you working your gift. We need all members working together like the fingers of the hand, each doing what he or she was assigned and designed to do!

We are in an intense battle with the forces of evil and are

greatly challenged as we seek to move forward with the plans and vision of God, and we need all members working their gifts to make us strong enough to conquer every foe. Can the body of Christ count on you?

CHAPTER 7
LESSONS FROM THE FIG TREE

He spake also this parable; A certain man had a fig tree planted in his vineyard; and he came and sought fruit thereon, and found none. ⁷ Then said he unto the dresser of his vineyard, Behold, these three years I come seeking fruit on this fig tree, and find none: cut it down; why cumbereth it the ground? ⁸ And he answering said unto him, Lord, let it alone this year also, till I shall dig about it, and dung it: ⁹ And if it bear fruit, well: and, if not, then after that thou shalt cut it down. (Luke 13:6–9)

The fig tree is a staple in Israel's history. It dates back to the beginning of mankind. It was obviously in the Garden of Eden, for it is mentioned for the first time in scripture in Genesis 3:7, where Adam and Eve, after they sinned, tried covering themselves with fig leaves.

The fig tree is the first fruit tree to be called by its proper name in scripture. Thus, it is one of the oldest and most long-standing trees to exist until this very day. What a mighty God and Creator we serve! Who can make a tree live and not become extinct for these many centuries?

There are more than 850 species of fig trees that have been cultivated for its edible fruit. Its God-ordained purpose is to continually produce edible fruit year after year. Thus, when Jesus sees a fig tree by the way bearing leaves, a strong indication that fruit was present, he is angered when he searches around the leaves and finds no fruit. Thus, he curses it, and the tree immediately withers and or dies (Matthew 21:18–20; Mark 11:12–14).

In the 13th chapter of St. Luke, leaves are not mentioned, but it can be safely assumed that this fig tree likewise has leaves but no fruit. The Master says that he has been looking for three years for fruit to grow on the tree, but nothing has happened. The tree gets as far as budding but stops growing. What is happening? Why is it not bearing fruit?

Let us make five observations from verses 8 and 9:

1. The Luke 13 fig tree is positioned in the Master's vineyard, where a vinedresser is employed to take care of the plants and trees planted there. The fig tree in the Gospels of Matthew and Mark is by the wayside and not identified with any Master; it has no vinedresser to speak up for it.

2. For three years, it has been promising fruit. Each year, it buds in the spring but brings forth no fruit (empty promises).

3. The Master classifies it as useless, unfit to any longer be a part of his vineyard. So, he orders it to be cut down.

4. The St. Luke fig tree has an advocate to speak up for it. The vinedresser says to his master, "Lord, let it alone this year also, till I shall dig about it, and dung it: And if it bear fruit, well: and if not, then after that thou shalt cut it down."

5. This fig tree is given one more year to prove that it can produce. It must never disappoint the master again. Next year this time, the master will be able to pluck figs from this tree and enjoy the nourishment they bring.

What if God gave each of us just one more year to account to Him for the gifts He has given to us? What if God said, "One year from now you must show me how effectively you have used my gifts to build, edify, and unify the body of Christ"?

Put yourself on this timeline and see how productive you can be within the next twelve months. What if your life depended upon it? Would you be diligent about it? Twelve months will fly by so fast; therefore, you must get started today. One of those gifts mentioned in the previous chapter is your gift. Work it!

CHAPTER 8
THE DOING FOLLOWS THE BEING

Be ye therefore followers of God, as dear children; and walk in love. Ephesians 5:1–2a

In Genesis chapter 1, we are made in God's image and after His likeness. In Genesis chapter 3, because of sin, we lost His likeness and marred His image. Thank God for Jesus, who came from heaven to earth to restore the image and likeness of God in us! God has predestinated us to be conformed to the image of His Son. This conformity takes place when we are born again.

We continue living out this predestinated course through the power of the Holy Spirit. We no longer live according to the dictates of the flesh but rather of the Spirit, who controls our God-ordained life!

- Be followers of God and then walk in love! The walking follows the being!

- Be holy and then do that which is right in the sight of the Lord! Doing follows being!

- Be transformed by renewing your mind then prove what is

that "good, acceptable, and perfect, will of God" (Romans 12:2).

What you do always follows your state of being! Tell me how you ought to be, and then I can tell you what you ought to do.

Be God-ordained, meaning that you are always God-conscious, always representing God, always bent on pleasing Him. To be ordained by God means that He positions and programs you to do His will. We are not indecisive. We "know whom [we] have believed, and [are] persuaded that he is able to keep that which [we] have committed unto him against that day" (2 Timothy 1:12).

So major in being what God has called you to be, and you will do what God wants you to do, for the doing follows the being.

CHAPTER 9

DON'T LOSE YOUR KEY OR YOUR PASSWORD!

Deeply embedded in the DNA of your God-ordained life is the key: your renewed mind that unlocks doors of wisdom and knowledge. With the mind, you serve the law of God (Romans 7:25). You are totally transformed by the renewing of your mind. God gave you this key of a sound mind. Through this sound mind, you have perfect peace and the ability and energy to strive together with other believers for the faith of the Gospel. And that is the password: faith in the Lord Jesus Christ.

With a renewed mind (the key) and faith (the password), you can carry out every assignment that God gives to you. For Christ strengthens your mind and your faith in order to equip you to do all things. Faith is the victory that overcomes the world (1 John 5:4). Jesus simply says to his disciples, "Have faith in God," and ye shall have whatever you say.

Faith must always be connected to someone infinitely more powerful than yourself. That someone is Jesus. I admonish you to exercise your faith by calling on His name, especially when you are in distress. For He is able to do exceeding abundantly above all that we ask or think, according to the power that works in us (Ephesians 3:20).

You see life now through a foggy lens. Only the Lord Jesus Christ sees clearly both your life and everything that impacts your life. For He sees the big picture, while you only see a clip. Thus, God sometimes causes you to wait for things you so greatly desire, knowing that a little adjustment now will bring great rewards later.

Go forth weeping bearing precious seed. Psalm 126:6 says that you will return rejoicing bringing sheaves with you. Please note the season of weeping and the season of rejoicing. Also, note that the end result is not the production of more seeds, but rather the copious generation of sheaves. Your reaping will be far greater than your sowing! It is God doing what HE and only HE can do that makes things come out right at the end. So, trust Him!

Job loses his children, cattle, and servants all in one day. He prays and sacrifices to God daily, and tragedy still comes his way. Why?

Answer: God knew that His servant Job could handle any negative life experience and that Job's faith in Him could be successfully tested even with the most extreme tragedy. Job loses material things but never loses his mind or his faith. Always keep your key and your password. When you read the end of his story, you will see that God uses Job's key and password to give him more after his trial of affliction than he had before.

Joseph simply obeys his father in going to see about his brothers and is thrown in a pit, sold into slavery and ends up a prisoner. What goes wrong?

Answer: Nothing! It was God's plan to separate him from his family, in order to place him into a position of destined national leadership in Egypt. He does not allow Potiphar's wife or anyone to sidetrack him and cause him to sin. He stays focused! He keeps his key and his password, and saves his entire family, including his father and his mean brothers.

Ruth is a faithful wife to her husband and a loyal daughter-in-law to Naomi, yet her husband dies before he can father a child by her, leaving her a widow in Moab. Could she have done something differently?

Answer: No! It is all in the plan of God to get Ruth from Moab to Bethlehem so that she can meet the man who would position her to be the progenitor of King David and eventually Jesus Christ, the promised Messiah. Ruth does not allow Orpah or Naomi to cause her to cast her key and password away.

She cleaves to her mother-in-law and says to Naomi, "Intreat me not to leave thee, or to return from following after thee: for whither thou goest, I will go; and where thou lodgest, I will lodge; thy people shall be my people, and thy God my God. Where thou diest, will I die, and there will I be buried; the Lord do so to me, and more also, if ought but death part thee and me" (Ruth 1:16–17).

When Naomi sees that Ruth is steadfastly minded to go with her, she drops the matter. The two of them leave Moab together and journey to Bethlehem, where God has everything planned and in order for both Naomi and Ruth. There, Ruth meets the wealthy Boaz, who becomes her redeemer and husband.

The end of the story sees Ruth married to Boaz and the exuberant mother of a son who later becomes the grandfather of the famous King David, thus making her his great-grandmother. Because of her roots in Moab, David uses it to his advantage when he is running for his life. He has friends in Moab and is able to leave his parents and family in a safe place in Moab until he can solidify his kingdom and personal safety. What a mighty God we serve!

Esther is an orphan (both mom and dad are dead), a Jewish captive in the Persian Kingdom, and part of the scattered remnant that does not return to Jerusalem under Ezra and Nehemiah. It is believed by some that those who did not return to Jerusalem were people who did not have the faith or courage to leave their relatively comfortable positions and residencies in Persia to face the potential hardships of the journey back home.

With Esther's parents deceased and no siblings to care for her, Mordecai, being the nephew of her father and a generation older than she, takes his cousin home with him to nurture her in the history of Israel and in the fear of the Lord. Thus, it is not Esther's fault that she is not in the number returning to Jerusalem. She never has the opportunity to do so. Why?

Such a beautiful girl, who should have been able to write her own ticket anywhere in the world, is stuck in a land of captivity, subject to the dictates of her elderly cousin and societal expectations. She was quickly becoming the product of her environment and the product of others' imagination, leaving her with few choices in life. The question is why?

Answer: She did not and could not at the time understand why she was fatherless and motherless and left subject to her elderly cousin in a land that was not considered her homeland. But God knew why. Note the continuation of the story.

After King Ahasuerus divorces his wife, Vashti, he begins the search for a new wife. He commissions a search committee to bring before him the most beautiful virgins in the province. Esther is one of those pretty virgins chosen to go through purification and to prepare to go before the king.

After a year of purification and preparation, the pretty girls, provided with whatever is thought to get the king's attention, parade before the king. None was chosen until the showing of Esther, who chooses to go before the king with only what is dictated to her by Hegai, the king's chamberlain and keeper of the women. The king loves her simple beauty and chooses her to be his wife. Who could imagine that a girl of foreign descent would end up being the queen of Persia? But when you have and use your key and password, anything can happen.

Since she likely was born in Sushan, she does not need to reveal her true heritage. She blends in so well with the Persian community that no questions are asked. So she is accepted by the king and his search committee without a racial roadblock.

Then the test of her life comes, when identifying with the Jewish people is inevitable. Haman, a high-ranking officer in the Persian kingdom, is an archenemy of the Jews. He develops an extreme hatred for Esther's cousin, Mordecai, who sits daily in the gate. Because Mordecai will not bow to Haman, Haman devises a plan to not only kill Mordecai, but to also kill his people, the Jews. He succeeds in getting the king to sign a petition authorizing the annihilation of all Jews in the Persian province.

Then Mordecai rents his clothes and puts on sackcloth with ashes. He goes outside the king's gate and cries bitterly in the streets. He then settles back at the king's gate, but this time outside the gate, for no one is allowed inside the king's gate in sackcloth. The Jewish people throughout the province join Mordecai in this public display of humiliation as they hear the petition being read about the day of their annihilation.

Esther's maids and chamberlains tell her what is happening

and reports that Mordecai is outside the gate in sackcloth. She immediately responds by sending Mordecai some new clothes, but Mordecai refuses the clothes. Then she calls for Hatach, the king's chamberlain whom the king had assigned to her, to go talk to Mordecai and find out what the problem is and why there is such a cry in the province.

Mordecai shares with Hatach about the petition that has been signed to annihilate the Jews. He gives Hatach a copy of the writing of the decree for him to give to Esther and tells him to give her a charge to go unto the king to make supplication and to make request before him for her people.

Hatach reports back to Esther all that Mordecai tells him. Esther sends Hatach back to Mordecai to say that the king has not called her in more than thirty days and that her life will be at risk if she approaches him, not having been called by him.

When Mordecai hears this, he sends a strong message to Esther, "Think not with thyself that thou shalt escape in the king's house, more than all the Jews. For if thou altogether holdest thy peace at this time, then shall there enlargement and deliverance arise to the Jews from another place; but thou and thy father's house shall be destroyed: and who knoweth whether thou art come to the kingdom for such a time as this?" (Esther 4:13–14).

Then Esther bids them to return to Mordecai and say, "Go, gather together all the Jews that are present in Shushan, and fast ye for me, and neither eat nor drink three days, night or day: I also and my maidens will fast likewise; and so will I go in unto the king, which is not according to the law: and if I perish, I perish" (Esther 4:16). Mordecai goes and does all that Esther commands him.

In the 5th chapter of Esther, she uses wisdom that only God could give her. She humbly approaches the king and is accepted by him. He asks what he can do for her, and she invites him and Haman, the Jews' enemy, to a banquet that day. The king accepts the invitation.

At the table the king asks Esther, "What is your petition?" (Esther 5:6). Esther responds with a second invitation for the king, along with Haman, to come to a special banquet the following day. She assures the king that she will tell him her petition at the next banquet. The king consents.

Haman goes home and reports to his wife and all his friends the glory he receives in being invited to the first banquet and that he has been invited to a second one on the next day. He speaks of all the honour that has been extended to him, and yet he is extremely unhappy as long as Mordecai sits outside the king's gate.

His wife and friends advises him to make a gallows seventy-five feet high, go to the king first thing tomorrow to get his approval for Mordecai to be hanged, and then go merrily into the second banquet. Haman does as they suggest. But watch God at work. He is always a step ahead of anything and everything Satan is planning for our destruction.

In chapter 6, during the course of the night, the king cannot sleep; so, he calls for his scribes, the keepers of records, and have them read before him. They read about Mordecai's report of a plot to destroy the king. The king asks, "What honour and dignity hath been done to Mordecai for this?" (Esther 6:3). The scribes say that nothing has been done.

Early in the morning, the king senses that someone is in the court. It is Haman, who has come to ask the king for Mordecai's death by hanging. But, before Haman can open his mouth, the king poses him with a question: "What shall be done unto the man whom the king delighteth to honour?" (Esther 6:6).

Haman can think only of himself as the man whom the king delights to honor. So he says,

> [8] Let the royal apparel be brought which the king useth to wear, and the horse that the king rideth upon, and the crown royal which is set upon his head: [9] And let this apparel and horse be delivered to the hand of one of the king's most noble princes, that they may array the man withal whom the king delighteth to honour, and bring him on horseback through the street of the city, and proclaim before

him, Thus shall it be done to the man whom the king delighteth to honour.

Esther 6:8–9

The king responds to Haman,

Make haste, and take the apparel and the horse, as thou hast said, and do even so to Mordecai the Jew, that sitteth at the king's gate: let nothing fail of all that thou has spoken.

Esther 6:10

Haman is crushed, but he has to act as if he is in total agreement or risk his own life. So, he departs and does as the king commands. It is the most humiliating assignment he has ever received.

He returns home and tells his wife and his friends what befalls him. The same people who had suggested he build a gallows for Mordecai now look at Haman as a falling star and predict his fall. Before he can finish his meeting with his wife and friends, the king's chamberlains are at the door to take Haman to the second banquet prepared by Queen Esther.

It is at this banquet that Esther has opportunity to tell the king her real petition. The king does not yet realize that the decree that he had signed will result in the destruction of Queen Esther's people. He is shocked to find out after several years of relating to Esther that she is of Jewish descent. The question then arises, who is the person who initiated this decree?

> [5] Then the king Ahasuerus answered and said unto
> Esther the queen, Who is he, and where is he, that
> durst presume in his heart to do so? [6] And Esther
> said, The adversary and enemy is this wicked
> Haman. Then Haman was afraid before the king
> and the queen.
>
> Esther 7:5–6

The king rises up in anger, and Haman justifiably fears for his life. The king leaves the banquet, and Haman falls into Esther's lap to beg for mercy. The king reenters and finds Haman on his wife's lap and immediately orders his arrest. A chamberlain tells the king about the gallows that Haman had built for Mordecai. The king then orders that Haman be hanged on that gallows the same day (Esther 7:7–10).

While Esther has his attention, she needs the king to undo the decree somehow. Thus, the king gives Mordecai the ring that Haman wore and gives Mordecai the authority to dictate a letter as he wishes, sealing it with the king's ring, so that whatever Haman had written would be nullified (Esther 8:2).

Now that Haman is deceased, the military has no one to give the order to go forward with the execution. Without touching the previously signed and sealed degree, the governing power is now in the hands of Mordecai the Jew to put the Jews in a position to destroy their enemies (Esther 8:9–13). The scribes are called in, and Mordecai works with them to get the wording just right before it is sealed and sent out to Jews in all 127 provinces of Persia.

There was great rejoicing in the camp of the Jews (Esther 8:16). God had miraculously turned their sorrow into joy and their mourning into dancing. What a mighty God we serve! He moves on behalf of people whose minds are stayed on him and who trust him! God gives total recovery to his people. Thank you, Lord!

Esther, Ruth, Joseph, and Job all had something in common. Each had a determined and focused mind (the key) and faith in the name of the Lord (the password).

> The name of the Lord is a strong tower: the righteous runneth into it, and is safe.
>
> Proverbs 18:10

> Some trust in chariots, and some in horses: but we will remember the name of the Lord our God.
>
> Psalm 20:7

> [14] Because he hath set his love upon me, therefore will I deliver him: I will set him on high, because he hath known my name. [15] He shall call upon me, and I will answer him: I will be with him in trouble; I will deliver him, and honour him. [16] With long life will I satisfy him, and shew him my salvation.
>
> Psalm 91:14–16

God miraculously blesses these biblical characters for not losing their key or their password. May God help you to make full use of your key and your password! DON'T LOSE THEM!

CHAPTER 10
BECOME "SIP" AND "SEE" WHOLE

Several years ago the Lord revealed to me His will for the whole man. He is not one-sided; He is concerned about all those things that concern us, from personal health to personal wealth, from the earthly to the heavenly. There is no concern that we have that God does not regard. He loves us!

I have worked with my SIP and SEE model for several years and have not found any human needs that do not fall within this model. While some of our needs are complex and fall partially in more than one class, every need that we have falls in at least one of the following categories:

Spiritual

Intellectual

Physical

Social

Emotional

Economical

It is my prayer that you will become SIP and SEE WHOLE!

THE SPIRITUAL NEED is a basic need from inception. It is God who made us; we didn't make ourselves. God breathed into man's nostrils the breath of life, and he became a living soul (Genesis 2:7). And it is in Him that "we live, and move, and have our being" (Acts 17:28). The only explanation for our continued existence is GOD! Our lives are totally dependent upon Him. Without Him, we "can do nothing" (John 15:5).

The twenty-four elders of Revelation 4:11 worship God with the words, "Thou art worthy, O LORD, to receive glory and honour and power: for thou hast created all things, and for thy pleasure they are and were created." Since all creation is for His pleasure, the psalmist says, "Let every thing that hath breath praise the Lord" (Psalm 150:6). But no one can genuinely praise or worship someone they don't know. Everyone needs a healthy understanding of who God is! So who is He?

> [23] Thus saith the Lord, Let not the wise man glory in his wisdom, neither let the mighty man glory in his might, let not the rich man glory in his riches: [24] But let him that glorieth glory in this, that he understandeth and knoweth me, that I am the Lord which exercise lovingkindness, judgment, and righteousness, in the earth: for in these things I delight, saith the Lord.
>
> Jeremiah 9:23-24

Apostle Paul gives Timothy a neat summary of who God is:

Now unto the King eternal, immortal, invisible, the only wise God, be honour and glory for ever and ever. Amen

1 Timothy 1:17

You will never get to the end of describing our great God. But this is a short version that we can memorize. So, when people ask you, "Who is GOD?", boldly say, "He is the King eternal, immortal, invisible, the only wise God."

The more we grasp this definition of God, the stronger our faith will be in Him, for the strength of our faith is directly proportionate to our clarity of understanding who God is. He is king eternal, always on the throne of this world, in full charge of everything. No one will ever unseat Him. It has been tried once; I am certain that it will not be tried again. Jesus said that He saw Satan fall out of heaven like lightning, for the fall was so quick. Satan lost his place in heaven forever. He can never regain his seat there.

The war of Armageddon as recorded in the 16th chapter of Revelation is the terrible and final conflict that Satan will have with God on earth (See also Zechariah 12:1–9 and Isaiah 10:28–32). This will be Satan's last and final stance. God will actively and visibly manifest His glorious power to the discomfiture and utter destruction of His enemies.

GOD IS KING ETERNAL, with unbroken age. He cannot be unseated.

HE IS IMMORTAL, that is to say, uncorrupted, imperishable, not liable to decay. He is not a product of our environment. HE is not affected by global warming. HE does not have the same atrophic principle working in Him that is working in all human beings. Atrophy is the natural process of wasting away, with the lessening of size and strength. It leads to loss of energy, eyesight, agility, mental capacity, and ability. At some point, most people will have the testimony of "the things I used to do, I don't do anymore." Atrophy ultimately leads to uselessness and finally death. Not so with God! He will never lose strength, size, mental capacity, sight, or ability. He is the same yesterday, today, and forever. Nothing changes Him from being who He is. He is God immortal!

HE IS THE INVISIBLE GOD. HE cannot be seen with the naked eye. He makes us, not we make him. So, when the heathen says, "Show us your God!", simply reply, "He is too great to show. His throne is far above the heavens. We cannot diminish Him to a sculpture to be held in one's hand."

And HE IS THE ONLY WISE GOD! There is no one who falls in His class. He stands alone as the one with unlimited wisdom and knowledge.

The purpose of Jesus coming into this world was to reveal God to us and to show us the extreme love that the Father has for us, which was evidenced by Him sending His only begotten Son into this world, not to condemn the world, but to save the world (John 3:17). The only thing we are required to do is believe on Him whom the father has sent.

One of Jesus' disciples asks, "Lord, shew us the Father." Jesus replies,

> [9] Have I been so long time with you, and yet hast thou not known me, Philip? he that hath seen me hath seen the Father; and how sayest thou then, Shew us the Father? [10] Believest thou not that I am in the Father, and the Father in me? the words that I speak unto you I speak not of myself: but the Father that dwelleth in me, he doeth the works.
>
> John 14:9–10

THE INTELLECTUAL NEED is married to the spiritual need, for the most talked about topic in all of history centers on God. For centuries, His name has been discussed on campuses around the world. So, we start with a comprehension of God.

Apostle Paul tells the Roman church "with the mind I myself serve the law of God; but with the flesh the law of sin" (Romans 7:25). Thus, there is a battle for the mind. Satan wants to corrupt our minds to prevent us from giving God the glory and honor He is due. Let us take another look at who God is, and never let anyone confuse you about His reality.

I still remember so clearly sitting in a philosophy class at UIC, when an interesting discussion came up about the existence of God. My class was taught by an agnostic professor who had earned two advanced degrees from the University of Chicago. On one particular day, she said, "Not that I believe that such a person exists (for I do not know what to believe), but, if there is a God, how must he be defined? Let's begin with some descriptive words about him."

You can imagine that this was probably the most exciting class I had in my college career. Here is a classroom of students preparing to define my God. Wow! How exciting!

If God is God, HE MUST BE ETERNALLY EXISTENT, one who has always existed, exists now, and will forever exist.

If God is God, HE MUST BE SELF-EXISTENT, never dependent on anything in the past, present or future. He must be God all by himself, not needing any props.

If God is God, HE MUST BE OMNISCIENT, one who knows all things in the infinite past, all things now, and all things in the infinite future.

If God is God, HE MUST BE OMNIPOTENT, one who was all-powerful in the infinite past, is all-powerful now, and will forever be all-powerful throughout the infinite future.

If God is God, HE MUST BE OMNIPRESENT, HE always

was and always will be. He is always HERE. HE is a walking HERE, a standard for all times!

If God is God, HE MUST BE TRANSCENDENT, so high above all powers that no competing power can touch Him.

If God is God, HE MUST BE IMMINENT, involved with the day-to-day governance of the universe.

In other words, God did not create the world and then go and hide, abandoning us earthbound creatures. HE is intricately involved with the affairs of humankind. God must be both transcendent and imminent.

Furthermore, God must be someone who is immutable (cannot be changed), incomprehensible (cannot be fully understood—our finite minds are too small to grasp the totality of his reality), invincible (cannot be defeated), and immeasurable (infinitely greater than anything or anyone we can imagine).

Finally, He must be one who fills heaven and earth, time and eternity, and space. He must be so high that no one can get over Him, so low that no one can go beneath Him, and so wide that no one can go around Him. In other words, He precedes all things in His priority, He exceeds all things in His superiority, and He succeeds all things in HIS finality. WHAT A MIGHTY GOD WE SERVE!

With the mind, we serve the law of God. Thus, we must be careful what we feed the mind. The mind forms images from words, songs, speech, drama, and the environment, and causes us to react emotionally, spiritually, physically, socially, or economically. The mind is the leading organ that coordinates all the other needs. The stem of the mind is the heart. Out of it flows the issues of life (Proverbs 4:23).

Man keeps trying to figure out or dismiss God. There was quite a stir one day at UIC when signs were placed throughout the college campus directing people to a certain lecture hall to hear a presentation from a visiting professor from the University of Chicago on the subject "God is dead!" Of course I was interested in hearing how anyone can prove that someone as real as my Heavenly Father is dead.

The lecture hall was filled to capacity. People were very interested in hearing the details of God's demise. I had never heard of this professor until now. He was totally unknown to me, yet I listened attentively as he very methodically proceeded to present the many arguments which support the non-existence of God. The entire hall of students and faculty seemed very swayed by these arguments.

Then came the surprise. The professor laid out the arguments for the existence of God and then said that it takes more faith to believe in the non-existence of God than to believe in His existence. The preponderance of evidence, universal design and order points to the reality and existence of GOD. He then announced that he was a believer and a Christian, because that which can be seen of God far outweighs the questions and doubts about Him.

How happy and relieved I was to hear his confession! Satan did not run away with the glory of that lecture. I simply wish someone could have introduced that audience to Jesus and made an altar call. I believe that several students would have responded to the gospel of Jesus Christ, because it is the power of God unto salvation to everyone that believes (Romans 1:16).

THE PHYSICAL NEED involves the well-being of the carrier of our soul. With the physical body we walk, talk, sing, play, work, interact, communicate, worship and praise God, and create. A well body performs far better than a sick one. Viruses and infections, the body's primary enemies, come to compromise the immune system.

We must do everything possible to maintain a strong immune system. Drink ample water, eat fruits and vegetables high in vitamin C, exercise, eat healthy, and get a minimum of six-to-eight hours of sleep each night. Do what you need to do to take care of yourself, and don't wait too long to seek professional medical help when needed. Why suffer longer than you need to?

My father became very ill one night. It was not like my father to be sick; he was always a picture of good health. But this night was different; he was really sick. He chose to go to the basement to suffer quietly, away from my mother. I did not understand then the misery he was enduring like I do now. I simply knew that I could not go to sleep when I knew my Dad was suffering like I had never known before.

So I would go to check on him hourly, asking him if he wanted me to call the doctor or take him to the hospital. The first few times he said that he didn't want medical attention. In other words, he thought that he could hold out; whatever was going on would pass. But it did not. So finally he said to me, "I do not think I can last much longer like this. Call the doctor." I called, and the doctor told me to get him to the hospital.

Dad moaned and groaned. I had never heard that of him before. I quietly helped him get dressed, got him in the car, and took him to the hospital, all while my mother remained asleep. He preferred not having a conversation regarding this matter because it was very private to him.

Now I am not trying to encourage men to keep personal issues from their wives, but there are times when men are not comfortable talking to their wives about their male issues. Of course, there are women who do not feel comfortable sharing female concerns with their husbands. In this case, it was personal. Mom did not have to get up in the middle of the night to accompany us to the hospital. I had Dad covered.

I got him registered in the emergency room, and shortly

thereafter they called him into an examination room. The pressure was so great that he could barely walk. I was in the waiting room for about forty minutes before I looked up and saw Dad walking toward me with a smile on his face. I immediately asked Dad, "Why did you wait so long, suffering needlessly, before seeking help?" He was so relieved that he did not even bother to respond. The medical staff did a simple procedure that gave him instant relief.

Sometimes we suffer with conditions longer than we need to. My father did not like going to the doctor. If he could get by on his own, he would do so as long as possible. I wonder are you that way? Are you holding out, not going to see a doctor for fear of what he/she might say or do? The relief you need could be a simple procedure, nothing complicated.

My advice is to go see the doctor, especially if you have been trying to deal with the problem on your own and nothing has changed for the better. Waiting too long may eventually complicate matters, leading to major surgery, when, if it had been addressed earlier, it would have required only a simple procedure.

Although we are a faith-based community, we believe God has equipped man with knowledge to help us get through some difficult challenges. Getting an annual physical is highly recommended and encouraged. Also health insurance can be a tremendous help in getting you the highest quality of health care services.

Also, do not underestimate the power of vitamins. There are

vitamins specific to men's health as well as to women's health. Vitamins can help fortify the body against physical attacks and can help the body's organs function more efficiently. Check into the science regarding vitamins and see what is right for you.

Last but not least, because we are the community of faith, we do believe in divine intervention. We pray one for the other that our bodies may be healed. God can do what medicines and vitamins cannot do. The Apostle James speaks of the elders anointing the sick with oil while praying effectually and fervently. "The prayer of faith shall save the sick, and the Lord will raise him up; and if he have committed sins, they shall be forgiven him" (James 5:14–16).

In my ministry, I maintain a supply of small bottles of oil that we bless in Jesus' name. We simply believe that the presence of God abides with this oil and that upon whomever it is used, he or she will receive healing and miracles that only God can do. The oil represents the prayers of the saints accompanying your faith to bring you the results you seek. It is us coming in agreement with you, touching something you desire on earth. Jesus says, "It shall be done for them of my Father which is in heaven" (Matthew 18:19). Are you saying, Yea, Lord, I believe?

THE SOCIAL NEED is the need to interact with others. No man is an island, and no man stands alone. We need one another for intellectual and emotional development, for friendship and for fellowship, for procreation and creation, for economic and physical development, etc. We together form a habitation for God. Thus, we need the Lord, and we need each other.

When Adam sinned, perfect harmony was lost. You never heard of a conflict in Adam and Eve's marriage until sin entered in. There was never an argument. The blame game began *after* they sinned. When God asks Adam, "Where are thou? ... Hast thou eaten of the tree, whereof I commanded thee that thou shouldest not eat?" Adam points his finger at Eve and says, "The woman whom thou gavest to be with me, she gave me of the tree, and I did eat" (Genesis 3:9, 11–12).

Adam neatly spreads the blame, placing it on the wife and on God. In essence he says, "It is the woman who gave the fruit to me, but it was you who gave the woman to me. So both of you are responsible for my failure."

Many conflicts have arisen in friendships and marriages because one party blamed another for his or her misfortunes. The sooner we can take responsibility for what comes our way, the sooner we can adapt to the present and begin creating a new chapter in our history. Do not waste valuable energy for months pointing fingers. This will only frustrate you more. Learn to say, "Okay, God, this is the situation. What would you have me to do now?" When you trust in the Lord with all [your] heart; and lean not [to your] own understanding and in all [your] ways acknowledge him, then he [will] direct [your] paths (Proverbs 3:5–6).

If you have a conflict with a family member or a church member, the Apostle Matthew instructs you to go to that person alone and show him or her the fault (Matthew 18:15). The fault is not something controversial but something clearly out of divine order, something the Holy Scriptures define as sinful.

In other words, we cannot challenge people about everything with which we disagree; we would never get through solving problems. Take the Word with you to be able to point out the need for corrective action. If you are successful, no one has to hear about it. Make sure you do not whisper to others about other people's faults. Try to cover with love as many faults as you can. Do not glory in the faults of others. You don't want others magnifying your faults, so don't magnify the faults of others.

If you are not successful at first, the scripture says to take one or two others with you as a witness to see if you can give understanding to the offender (Matthew 18:16). Again, if successful, nothing else needs to be said or done. Resolve conflict at the lowest level possible.

Most issues should never come before the entire church. Only when the above process does not work can you then choose to bring the matter to the church. Again, remember that bringing a matter to the entire church is a serious matter. If handled with insensitivity, souls could be damaged for years to come. Make this the FINAL STEP after all else fails.

A good rule of thumb is to keep small matters small. Do not make mountains out of molehills. Give the attention necessary to resolve the heavy matters, always operating in love and sensitivity, and try to break heavy or complicated matters into smaller, more manageable pieces. Some problems can be handled better in bite-sized packages than altogether.

It has been said that a friend is hard to find. Yet, the wise man Solomon says that if you want friends, show yourself friendly (Proverbs 18:24). Be courteous, kind, hospitable, and empathetic to others, and the love you extend to others will come back to you. Do not let a bad experience turn you off to all people. Bad experiences make us more cautious going forward, but they should not and must not stop us from forming new, healthy relationships. Ask God to guide you in this area.

Finally, restoration must precede reconciliation. God had to work with Esau and Jacob separately before they could come together peacefully. By the time they finally came together, each had been internally restored. Past issues were forgiven, and they were ready for the reunion.

When you have two bitter factions, pray that God will restore unto each the joy of their salvation and the wisdom and peace to release the offense of the past. Then pray for reconciliation. Without restoration, there will be no true reconciliation.

THE EMOTIONAL NEED involves our feelings, our mental inclinations, our drive, our passions, our fears, our lusts, and our strong desires. This is the most difficult area of our lives to satisfy. Once our flesh gets what it wants, it not long thereafter will want something else and then something else. Thus, it is foolish and unreasonable to expect another human being to satisfy all your emotional needs. You are living in a fantasy world if you imagine meeting Mr. Right or Ms. Suitable and having him or her be able to perfectly satisfy all of your emotional needs.

It is true, however, that the right person can make you emotionally whole. Some people are depositors to your emotional bank account; others are drainers to your account. When talking to some people, you feel refreshed, renewed, and reenergized. When talking to others, you feel drained, wiped out, zapped, and depleted.

Lord, spare us from the drainers! The truth is you cannot avoid drainers all the time. You must daily replenish yourself, get fortified for the challenges of the new day, and be prepared to deal with the drainers assigned to you.

While there are many suggestions for replenishing self (read a good book, listen to relaxing music, take a vacation, take a boat trip, go fishing, golfing, swimming, dancing, meditating, etc.), Jesus showed His disciples the primary way that He replenished himself.

Note in Matthew 14:23, Mark 6:46, Luke 6:12 and 9:28 that Jesus goes up into a mountain to pray. Mark 1:35 says He went into a solitary place. Luke 5:16 says He went into the wilderness and prayed. Luke 11:1 says He went in to a certain place to pray. Each time, He went away from the crowd to spend time with the Father.

In Luke 18:1, Jesus "spake a parable to this end, that men ought always to pray, and not to faint." First Thessalonians 5:17 says, "Pray without ceasing." Our greatest replenishment will come through stealing away to pray.

Are you a depositor or a drainer in the emotional account of your spouse, children, siblings, relatives, friends, schoolmates, parishioners, and associates? Do you see your presence adding something positive to your environment or taking away? Is the fellowship going to be enriched or drained by your presence? Will the church be edified or crushed by your ministry?

Since emotions involve our passions (that drive and willingness to do whatever is necessary to reach a specific goal), we must make sure that its train is on the right track to get us to where we want to go. The word of God is a lamp unto our feet and a light in our path (Psalm 119:105).

It is easy to become emotionally bent out of shape when you are not feeling appreciated or understood by someone close to you. Resentment and bitterness can set in when only negative things are being deposited in you. Resentment and bitterness can also develop when you try unsuccessfully to please the person you love. You have to war against bitterness because it will defile you and hurt others. The right way to respond is to overcome evil with good. Always do well and remember that it is never wrong to do right and never right to do wrong!

Keeping a handle on our emotions can be a challenge because Satan uses various tactics to discourage us, make us feel defeated, useless, worthless, inadequate, and helpless, or he uses them to make us greedy for power or positions, lustful for immediate fleshly gratification, or proud, seeking vain glory. The enemy will surround you with individuals who carry these emotionally draining spirits to influence your spirit. Know the words of the longstanding hymn by Horatio R. Palmer:

> "Yield not to temptation, for yielding is sin.
> Each victory will help you, some others to win.
> Fight manfully onward; Dark passions subdue.
> Look ever to Jesus, and He will carry you through.
> Shun evil companions; bad language disdain.
> God's name hold in reverence; nor take it in vain.
> Be thoughtful and earnest, kindhearted and true.
> Look ever to Jesus, and He will carry you through.
> To him that overcomes, God gives a crown.
> Through faith, we will conquer, though often cast down.
> He who is our Savior, our strength will renew.
> Look ever to Jesus, and He will carry you through.
> Ask the Savior to help you, comfort, strengthen, and keep you.
> He is willing to aid you. He will carry you through."

It is when you are emotionally vulnerable that Satan comes so strongly, with temptation masked as a means of relief from the pain, the misery, the loneliness, and the disappointment. He thinks he can render a fatal blow while we are less likely to resist him. But declare with me: "I am stronger at my weakest moment than Satan is at his strongest." Paul, in encouraging the church at Corinth, declares: "When I am weak, then am I strong" (2 Corinthians 12:10). The prophet Joel puts it this way: "Let the weak say, I am strong" (Joel 3:10).

I still hear the remorseful caller to a Moody Talk Show who told the story of a season of broken communication between him and his wife. They were not talking. They were not at all seeking to meet each other's needs. So in a moment of frustration, he decided to step outside of his marriage for one moment of instant gratification. I can still hear his weeping voice saying, "Just one time I stepped outside my marriage. I felt justified because my wife was cold toward me. Just one time," he repeated, "I was unfaithful, and now I have AIDS!"

Just one time! That's all it takes to get a sexually transmitted disease. If the enemy has been tempting you to be unfaithful to God, resist him steadfastly. Make him flee. He is trying to kill you. This is not a game; this is his destructive strategy. But you must "fight the good fight of faith, lay hold on eternal life" (1 Timothy 6:12).

If the enemy was successful in getting you to yield to his ploy, thank God that the disease and the full consequence of your action was not realized. That is what mercy is, preventing you from receiving what you rightly deserve. You should turn to God now with a heart of gratitude, and promise to obey Him and to keep His commandments. You will no longer let emotions rule you. From this day forward, you will rule your emotions.

Concerning the young man with AIDS, is there any hope for him? Thank God, I am a preacher of the gospel! There is hope for him! Emphatically, yes, there is hope for him and all who have been ensnared by Satan.

> [6] Blessed be the Lord, who hath not given us as a prey to their teeth. [7] Our soul is escaped as a bird out of the snare of the fowlers: the snare is broken, and we are escaped. [8] Our help is in the name of the Lord, Who made heaven and earth.
>
> Psalm 124:6–8

We worship and serve one who is able to break the snare! There is nothing too hard for him. There is nothing impossible for him. "With God all things are possible" (Matthew 19:26; Mark 10:27).

God invites us to "come boldly unto the throne of grace," where we can "obtain mercy, and find grace to help in time of need" (Hebrews 4:16). I envision a church with a Throne of Grace Prayer Chapel, where people from around the world can come and experience the mercy and grace of God.

We cannot heal AIDS, but God can! We may be so deep in debt that we cannot swim out, but God knows the way out. There are times, because of our own misbehavior, when we find ourselves in a deep hole, but God can get us out! GOD STILL WORKS MIRACLES!

I love the 107th Psalm, where the psalmist says,

> [17] Fools because of their transgression, and because of their iniquities, are afflicted. [18] Their soul abhorreth all manner of meat; and they draw near unto the gates of death. [19] Then they cry unto the Lord in their trouble, and he saves them out of their distresses. [20] He sent his word, and healed them, and delivered them from their destructions. [21] Oh that men would praise the Lord for his goodness, and for his wonderful works to the children of men!
>
> Psalm 107:17–21

THE ECONOMIC NEED has always been challenging. For most of us, we probably spend more time thinking about this need than any other need because everything costs money. Money answers all things (Ecclesiastes 10:19). "Money" can be found 189 times in the Bible. The Holy Scriptures are clear on how to get money, spend money, and save money. Consider these:

HOW TO GET IT!

➤ "In the sweat of thy face shalt thou eat bread" (Genesis 3:19). You will have to work hard to eat.

➤ [10b] We beseech you, brethren, that ye increase more and more;[11] And that ye study to be quiet, and to do your own business, and to work with your own hands, as we commanded you; [12] That ye may walk honestly toward them that are without, and that ye may have lack of nothing" (1 Thessalonians 4:10b–12).

Note the words of Solomon in the book of Proverbs:

➢ 10:4 - "He becometh poor that dealeth with a slack hand: but the hand of the diligent maketh rich."

➢ 12:24 - "The hand of the diligent shall bear rule: but the slothful shall be under tribute."

➢ 14:4 - "Where no oxen are, the crib is clean: but much increase is by the strength of the ox"

➢ 13:4 - "The soul of the sluggard desireth, and hath nothing: but the soul of the diligent shall be made fat."

➢ 21:5 - "The thoughts of the diligent tend only to plenteousness, but of every one that is hasty only to want."

➢ 22:29 - "Seest thou a man diligent in his business? He shall stand before kings; he shall not stand before mean [low, insignificant] men."

➢ 27:23 - "Be thou diligent to know the state of thy flocks, and look well to thy herds."

What do you have working for you? Name your ox! Jesus

suggested that a good way to increase money is by trading (Luke 19:15). The least we can do is put it in the bank to gain some interest. In Matthew 25:27, we find this exhortation: "… put my money to the exchangers." In other words, put money in the hands of people in the business of turning money into profit. Deuteronomy 14:25 and Acts 4:37 both suggest turning real estate into money, when it is needed for a good purpose.

Giving your way into major increase is another avenue that should always be explored!

> ⁶ But this I say, He which soweth sparingly shall reap also sparingly; and he which soweth bountifully shall reap also bountifully. ⁷ Every man according as he purposeth in his heart, so let him give; not grudgingly, or of necessity: for God loveth a cheerful giver. ⁸ And God is able to make all grace abound toward you; that ye, always having all sufficiency in all things, may abound to every good work (2 Corinthians 9:6–8).

> ⁵ They that sow in tears shall reap in joy. ⁶ He that goeth forth and weepeth, bearing precious seed, shall doubtless come again with rejoicing, bringing his sheaves with him (Psalm 126:5–6).

> Give, and it shall be given unto you; good measure, pressed down, and shaken together, and running over, shall men give into your bosom. For with the same measure that ye mete withal it shall be measured to you again (Luke 6:38).

➤ [7] Return unto me, and I will return unto you, saith the Lord of hosts. But ye said, Wherein shall we return? [8] Will a man rob God? Yet ye have robbed me. But ye say, Wherein have we robbed Thee? In tithes and offerings. [9] Ye are cursed with a curse: for ye have robbed me, even this whole nation. [10] Bring ye all the tithes into the storehouse, that there may be meat in mine house, and prove me now herewith, said the Lord of hosts, if I will not open you the windows of heaven, and pour you out a blessing, that there shall not be room enough to receive it. [11] And I will rebuke the devourer for your sakes, and he shall not destroy the fruits of your ground; neither shall your vine cast her fruit before the time in the field, said the Lord of hosts. [12] And all nations shall call you blessed: for ye shall be a delightsome land, said the Lord of hosts" (Malachi 3:7–12).

➤ [17] And it shall come to pass after the end of seventy years, that the Lord will visit Tyre, and she shall turn to her hire, and shall commit fornication with all the kingdoms of the world upon the face of the earth. [18] And her merchandise and her hire shall be holiness to the Lord: it shall not be treasured nor laid up; for her merchandise shall be for them that dwell before the LORD, to eat sufficiently, and for durable clothing" (Isaiah 23:17–18).

HOW TO SPEND IT!

PRIORITIZE your spending:

> ➤ God first (tithes: 10% minimum)
>
> ➤ Yourself second (savings: 10%)
>
> ➤ Free will offering to church, charities, people in need, special needs, etc. (10%)
>
> ➤ Basic necessities (food, shelter, utilities, education, transportation, debts, etc.: 60%)
>
> ➤ Recreation (spending money: 10%)

Consider these scriptures for instruction:

> ➤ And thou shalt bestow that money for whatsoever thy soul lusteth after ... (Deuteronomy 14:26). God promises and gives us spending money if we do what He has commanded us to do. Note that the 25th verse encourages turning real estate into money. If we get this balance right, God is going to give us spending money!
>
> ➤ 24 There is that scattereth, and yet increaseth; and there is that withholdeth more than is meet, but it tendeth to poverty. 25 The liberal soul shall be made fat: and he that watereth shall be watered also himself (Proverbs 11:24–25).
>
> ➤ Owe no man any thing, but to love one another: for he that loveth another hath fulfilled the law (Romans 13:8).

HOW TO SAVE IT!

> ➤ "A good man leaves an inheritance to his children's children: and the wealth of the sinner is laid up for the just (Proverbs 13:22).

Remember the model above regarding saving 10% of every increase! My father used to say that if you put a penny away every day and do not touch it, it will be there for you when you need it. So, put away 10% and spend it only in an emergency or only if you know that within a few days, additional funds will be coming to you and you can replace what was taken out. Do not spend money simply because you have money to spend. That is wasting money. Put every dollar to good use. There is no end to all the stuff you can buy in this world. Be selective in your spending and save as much as you can for more big-ticket items or a vacation.

COMMON SENSE MONEY PRINCIPLES TO LIVE BY

1. INCOME > EXPENSES = PROFIT
2. PROFIT + WISE MANAGEMENT = SAVINGS
3. EXPENSES > INCOME = DEFICIT
4. EXPENSES = INCOME = NOTHING
5. Never lend to anyone money you need to live on. This means never lend your mortgage or rent money to anyone, no matter how desperate they are. Better to hand them a gift of a few dollars than to hear the borrower tell you

why he or she cannot repay you when the due date arrives. Then what are you going to do? Strangling them will not get you any money.

6. Success in trading:

    a. trade often and make small gains

    b. win more than you lose

    c. sometimes win big

7. An ounce of prevention is better than a pound of cure!

NEVER UNDERESTIMATE the POWER of a PENNY!

Let us try a fun exercise called The Matching Gift:

1. Starting on a Sunday, place a penny in a large cup or jar.

2. The next day, match what is in the cup or jar.

Can you keep this going for fourteen days, twenty-one days, or thirty days? See how far you can go. This could be your savings strategy, for you can restart this cycle as often as you'd like. Are you surprised at how quickly a penny can turn into hundreds and thousands of dollars?

What if we do this for the building of God's kingdom? Can we ask God to increase our faith and help us to go further than we ever thought we could go? This exercise ends on the day that you are no longer able to match what's in the jar/cup. I would suggest that you wait a week or two before starting the exercise again. This time, see if you can go further than the first time.

CHAPTER 11
I BLESS YOU IN THE NAME OF THE LORD!

And the Lord spake unto Moses, saying, ²³ Speak unto Aaron and unto his sons, saying, On this wise ye shall bless the children of Israel, saying unto them, ²⁴ The Lord bless thee, and keep thee: ²⁵ The Lord make his face shine upon thee, and be gracious unto thee: ²⁶ The Lord lift up his countenance upon thee, and give thee peace. ²⁷ And they shall put my name upon the children of Israel; and I will bless them. (Numbers 6:22–27)

God says if I stamp His name on you with the words which He has given, He will bless you. Are you ready for this blessing?

Please note that everything that takes place in the first six chapters is designed to bring divine order among God's people in the earth. The children of Israel were chosen to be a peculiar people unto the Lord. They were required to walk differently than the heathens. They could not operate by the rules of the heathen nations. God has his own laws, and he expects his people to obey.

Chapter 6 begins with the rules governing men or women who choose to separate themselves to the Lord through a vow of a Nazarite: 1) must not shave his/her hair, 2) must not take any wine, vinegar, or strong drink, 3) must not eat any grapes, 4) must not come near a dead body, even if it is his/her mother, father, sibling, child, etc., and 5) must offer sacrifices to the Lord and make himself/herself available for whatever service the priest might assign to him/her.

Men and women voluntarily consecrated themselves before God. This was their way of drawing near to God. They set the time or duration for their consecration; however, the shortest time known is thirty days. Thus, anyone making this vow would be consecrating themselves for at least thirty days. After this comes the closing blessing.

Are you understanding that the blessing is about to be administered to a people who have a strong sense of consecration and commitment to the Lord? Thus, God says to Moses, stamp my name on these people! If you put my name on them, I will bless them!

So, prepare yourself now to receive this blessing by saying, "Lord, I dedicate myself to You. Whatever You want me to do, I will do it. I sanctify myself of every corrupt way and unclean habit to serve You, Lord. Wash me in the blood of Jesus and fill me with Your Holy Spirit. Be the Lord of my life. And I'll love You, I'll serve You, I'll praise You all the days of my life. Thank You, Lord, for hearing my prayer!" With that, you are ready, and I am ready to stamp God's name on you. Let us get started.

"THE LORD BLESS YOU AND KEEP YOU!"

The Lord congratulates you on your move toward Him. He welcomes you into His presence and invites you to fullness of joy and pleasures evermore. The Lord bless you and watch over you, protecting you, paying close attention to your well-being, and keeping you on track for victorious living!

I pray that as God comforted Moses in Exodus 23:20, saying, "Behold, I send an Angel before thee, to keep thee in the way [to preserve thee in the journey], and to bring thee into the place which I have prepared," that He will give His Angels charge over you, keeping you in all your ways. May they bear you up, lest you dash your foot against a stone!

Furthermore, the Lord who made heaven and earth, the world and all that dwell therein "[sits] upon the circle of the earth, and the inhabitants thereof are as grasshoppers." He "[stretches] out the heavens as a curtain, and [spreads] them out as a tent to dwell in" (Isaiah 40:22).

"The everlasting God, the Lord, the Creator of the ends of the earth, fainteth not, neither is weary? There is no searching of his understanding. He giveth power to the faint; and to them that have no might he increaseth strength. Even the youths shall faint and be weary, and the young men shall utterly fall: But they that wait upon the Lord shall renew their strength; they shall mount up with wings as eagles; they shall run, and not be weary; and they shall walk, and not faint" (Isaiah 40:28–31). Therefore, I encourage you to "wait on the Lord: be of good courage, and he shall strengthen thine heart: wait, I say, on the LORD" (Psalm 27:14).

"THE LORD MAKE HIS FACE SHINE UPON YOU, AND BE GRACIOUS UNTO YOU!"

May the Lord smile upon you and favor you! May the Lord deal kindly and graciously with you! The Lord's face is toward you. He will not turn his back to you. He will never leave you nor forsake you. He promises to be with you always, even unto the end of the world (Matthew 28:20). Amen!

"For God, Who commanded the light to shine out of darkness, hath shined in our hearts, to give the light of the knowledge of the glory of GOD in the face of JESUS CHRIST" (2 Corinthians 4:6).

"THE LORD LIFT UP HIS COUNTENANCE UPON YOU, AND GIVE YOU PEACE!"

I pray that the Lord will uncover His face to you and show you His favor. I pray that He will look kindly upon you and give you an abundance of peace. I pray that the Lord will prosper your way and grant you total confidence and trust in Him.

May the "grace of the Lord Jesus Christ, and the love of God, and the communion of the Holy Ghost, be with you all! Amen" (2 Corinthians 13:14).

"The grace of our Lord Jesus Christ be with you all! Amen" (Revelation 22:21).

THE AFTERGLOW

I was at a personal development workshop many years ago, where I met the author of the poem entitled "The Race!" He quoted it from memory, which made a major impact on this class of middle-to-upper management professionals. It was a great way to send us home.

Used by permission of the author, Dr. D. H. (Dee) Groberg

THE RACE

By Dr. D.H. (Dee) Groberg

I

"Quit! Give Up! You're beaten!"
They shout at me and plead.
"There's just too much against you now.
This time you can't succeed."

And as I start to hang my head
In front of failure's face,
My downward fall is broken by
The memory of a race.

And hope refills my weakened will
As I recall that scene;
For just the thought of that short race
Rejuvenates my being.

II

A children's race—young boys, young men—
How I remember well.
Excitement, sure! But also fear;
It wasn't hard to tell.

They all lined up so full of hope
Each thought to win that race.
Or tie for first, or if not that,
At least take second place.

And fathers watched from off the side
Each cheering for his son.
And each boy hoped to show his dad
That he would be the one.

The whistle blew and off they went
Young hearts and hopes afire.
To win and be the hero there
Was each young boy's desire.

And one boy in particular
Whose dad was in the crowd
Was running near the lead and thought:
"My did will be so proud!"

But as they speeded down the field
Across a shallow dip,
The little boy who thought to win
Lost his step and slipped.

Trying hard to catch himself
His hands flew out to brace,
And mid the laughter of the crowd
He fell flat on his face.

So down he fell and with him hope
–He couldn't win it now–
Embarrassed, sad, he only wished
To disappear somehow.

But as he fell his dad stood up
And showed his anxious face,
Which to the boy so clearly said,
"Get up and win the race."

He quickly rose, no damage done,
–Behind a bit, that's all–

And ran with all his mind and might
To make up for his fall.

So anxious to restore himself
–To catch up and to win–
His mind went faster than his legs:
He slipped and fell again!

He wished then he had quit before
With only one disgrace.
"I'm hopeless as a runner now;
I shouldn't try to race."

But in the laughing crowd he searched
And found his father's face;
That steady look which said again:
"Get up and win the race!"

So up he jumped to try again
–Ten yards behind the last–
"If I'm to gain those yards," he thought,
"I've got to move real fast."

Exerting everything he had
He regained eight or ten,
But trying so hard to catch the lead
He slipped and fell again!

Defeat! He lied there silently
–A tear dropped from his eye–
"There's no sense running anymore;
Three strikes: I'm out! Why try!"

The will to rise had disappeared;
All hope had fled away;
So far behind, so error prone;
A loser all the way.

"I've lost, so what's the use," he thought
"I'll live with my disgrace."
But then he thought about his dad
Who soon he'd have to face.

"Get up," an echo sounded low.
"Get up and take your place;
You were not meant for failure here.
Get up and win the race."

"With borrowed will get up," it said,
"You haven't lost at all.
For winning is no more than this:
To rise each time you fall."

So up he rose to run once more,
And with a new commit

He resolved that win or lose
At least he wouldn't quit.

So far behind the others now,
–The most he'd ever been–
Still he gave it all he had
And ran as though to win.

Three times he'd fallen, stumbling;
Three times he rose again;
Too far behind to hope to win
He still ran to the end.

They cheered the winning runner
As he crossed the line first place.
Head high, and proud, and happy;
No falling, no disgrace.

But when the fallen youngster
Crossed the line last place,
The crowd gave him the greater cheer,
For finishing the race.

And even though he came in last
With head bowed low, unproud,
You would have thought he'd won the race
To listen to the crowd.

And to his dad he sadly said,
"I didn't do too well."
"To me, you won," his father said.
"You rose each time you fell."

III

And now when things seem dark and hard
And difficult to face,
The memory of that little boy
Helps me in my race.

For all of life is like that race,
With ups and downs and all.
And all you have to do to win,
Is rise each time you fall.

"Quit! Give up! You're beaten!"
They still shout in my face.
But another voice within me says:
"GET UP AND WIN THE RACE!"

This is the original copywritten version of "The Race"

STATEMENTS OF CONTRIBUTION

This book shares the keys to a God-ordained life. Through specific application of scriptures, Bishop Austin exhorts you not only to stay on course, but also to finish well. ~

Dr. Darnell L. Thomas, Projects Administrator, Chicago Department of Public Health

The God-Ordained Life is a book of spiritual tidbits that will trigger readers to critically evaluate their obedience in both hearing the word of God and doing the will of God. Bishop James C. Austin, Sr. expounds upon biblical truths that capture the very essence of a life that is set apart by God. ~

Dr. Carol Y. Collum, Founder and CEO of True Believers Community Connections

I served under the ministry leadership of Bishop Austin for twenty-three years and I am overjoyed at this great accomplishment. Bishop Austin is one of the most astute, profound orators of the gospel of Jesus Christ, and finally he is showcasing his brilliance in print. Bishop Austin penned a song, "God's Tomorrow is Better than Today." Well, Bishop Austin, "God's Tomorrow" is now your today. Thank you for sharing your God-given talents. ~

Dr. Jonathan Shepherd, Board Certified Child, Adolescent, and Adult Psychiatrist

Bishop James C. Austin, Sr. is a generous, hospitable man of God who teaches practical biblical applications in a dynamic and relatable manner. *The God-Ordained Life* is a collection of thought provoking, faith building stories and scriptural truths written in a unique and conversational style. This book should inspire you to do greater works! ~

Dr. Astead N. Herndon, Former Adjunct Professor at Wheaton College and Trinity International University

The God-Ordained Life is a power-packed devotional that is filled with great Scripture quotes, vivid images, and solid life applications. An inspiring text, it will encourage many in living fully the Christian life. ~

Bishop David Daniels, III, Henry Winters Luce Professor of World Christianity, McCormick Theological Seminary, Chicago

Our dad has always been one with practical wisdom for life. His preaching mirrors his daily instructions to live wisely, be optimistic, and maintain an enduring faith in God. You will enjoy reading the wisdom that comes from the biblical text, creation, and life itself. ~

The Children: Atty. James Jr., Dorcas (MA Harvard), Prisca (BA Loyola), and Marcus (BA Rutgers).

ABOUT THE AUTHOR

Bishop **James Curtis Austin, Sr.** is a dedicated pastor, spiritual teacher, and uncompromising preacher of the gospel of Jesus Christ. He is known and respected as an honorable man, a holy man, a man of God. He is the husband of Missionary Vernesta T. Austin. Together, they are the proud parents of James, Jr., Dorcas, Prisca, and Marcus.

Bishop Austin received his call to ministry in 1966 and graduated in 1967 from the University of Illinois with a Bachelor of Science Degree. In 1978, he was appointed Pastor of the St. Luke Church of God in Christ and was consecrated to the sacred office of Bishop in 2004. The church was located in the notorious and troubled Cabrini-Green Community, which is a little over one mile north of City Hall and downtown Chicago. This proximity allowed him to establish longstanding affiliations with local organizations such as Tabitha House (a home for the homeless) and the renowned Moody Bible Institute.

It was through these partnerships that he unyieldingly performed acts of kindness and made contributions to underserved and underprivileged individuals in this near north community and around the world. Public officials such as former Illinois Governor Pat Quinn, President Barack Obama (then Senator), and Illinois Secretary of State Jesse White have visited St. Luke because of its reputation and notability in Chicago.

Bishop Austin is a visionary leader. His extraordinary leadership abilities are exemplified in his major contributions to the kingdom of God. He is the founder of For Christ Ministries, Inc., where he was instrumental in planting international ministries in the Republic of Trinidad/Tobago. He is currently the Vice-President of the Near North Ministry Alliance, where he guides a panel of members that represent eight denominations toward the common goal of addressing community concerns. He also served as a member of the Board of Directors of the National Charles Harrison Mason Foundation and as Vice-President of the Olive Branch Mission (a shelter for the homeless). Under his direction, the body of Christ is crossing cultural boundaries, resolving family and community crisis, and coming to a renewed faith in Jesus Christ.

One of Bishop Austin's most profound accomplishments was producing *The Legacy of a Leader*, which is a commemorative video documentary on the life of the late Bishop Charles Harrison Mason, the most unsung hero of the 20th Century. Bishop Austin continues unto this day as a servant of the Lord Jesus Christ and as a faithful minister to God's people.

For more information regarding Bishop James C. Austin, Sr. and his ministry, please refer to THE GOD-ORDAINED LIFE website: www.thegodordainedlife.com.

About the Publisher

Let us bring your story to life! With Life to Legacy, we offer the following publishing services: manuscript development, editing, transcription services, ghostwriting, cover design, copyright services, ISBN assignment, worldwide distribution, and eBooks.

Throughout the entire production process, you maintain control over your project. We are here to serve you. Even if you have no manuscript at all, we can ghostwrite your story for you from audio recordings or legible handwritten documents.

We also specialize in family history books, so you can leave a written legacy for your children, grandchildren, and others. You put your story in our hands, and we'll bring it to literary life! We have several publishing packages to meet all your publishing needs.

Call us at: 877-267-7477, or you can also send e-mail to: Life2Legacybooks@att.net. Please visit our website:

www.Life2Legacy.com

CPSIA information can be obtained at www.ICGtesting.com
Printed in the USA
LVOW12s0725080615

441558LV00003B/5/P